No Nonsense English

10–11 years

D0491825

Contents

www.bond11plus.co.uk

Handwriting practice

Copy this poem on the lines underneath.

The Pobble who has no toes

The Pobble who has no toes
Had once as many as we;
When they said "Some day you may lose them all;"
He replied "Fish, fiddle-de-dee!"
And his Aunt Jobiska made him drink
Lavender water tinged with pink,
For she said "The World in general knows
There's nothing so good for a Pobble's toes!"

Copy this piece of writing on the lines underneath.

Treasure Island

I remember him as if it were yesterday. He came plodding to the inn door – a tall, strong, heavy, nut-brown man, his tarry pigtail falling over the shoulder of his soiled blue coat, his hands ragged and scarred, with black, broken nails, and the sabre cut across one cheek. I remember him breaking out in that old sea-song that he sang so often afterwards: "Fifteen men on the dead man's chest – Yo-ho-ho, and a bottle of rum!"

More practice? Go to www

Lesson 1 Spelling

Unstressed vowels

Unstressed vowels are either:
- not sounded clearly, e.g. the second 'a' in par**a**llel (it sounds like 'uh')

OR
- not sounded at all, e.g. the 'e' in geography.

QUICK TIP!
Use a dictionary to look up any spellings you are unsure about.

1. Say these words and underline the unstressed vowels.

a fattening **b** dandelion **c** miniature **d** interest **e** astronomy

f abandon **g** lettuce **h** benefit **i** journalist **j** mathematics

2. Write the unstressed vowels in these words.

a tel__vision **b** parli__ment **c** alc__hol **d** cons__n__nt **e** d__scribe

f loc__motive **g** sign__ture **h** med__cine **i** sim__lar **j** gramm__r

3. These words have unstressed vowels in them. Underline the words that are spelt correctly.

a separate seperate **b** definate definite **c** intresting interesting

d teluphone telephone **e** vegtable vegetable **f** secrutry secretary

g holiday holuday **h** confrunce conference **i** lemonade lemunade

4. When a word ending in ary, ery or ory is spoken it can be hard to tell how to spell the ending. Write the words in the correct columns depending upon their endings.

(5 marks)

Words		ary endings	ery endings	ory endings
lott _ _ _	Febru _ _ _			
hist _ _ _	Janu _ _ _			
fact _ _ _	bound _ _ _			
categ _ _ _	station _ _ _			
volunt _ _ _	jewell _ _ _			
batt _ _ _	veterin _ _ _			

QUICK TIP!
One word belongs in two columns. Which word is it?

0 Tough OK Got it! 35

Total /35

More practice? Go to 

Word roots

Many words, such as **pay** or **day**, can be used as root words. Prefixes or suffixes can be added to a root word to create a new word:

repay **payment**

Sometimes the new words will be compound words:

daylight **birthday**

1. Find the root word hidden inside the longer word. The first one has been done for you.

a indigestible	concept		**b** decipherable	learn
c preferential	valid		**d** hyphenated	integrate
e invalidity	digest		**f** disintegration	cipher
g misconception	prefer		**h** unlearned	hyphen

2. Write three new words using each root word.

a work ______ ______ ______

b side ______ ______ ______

c some ______ ______ ______

d post ______ ______ ______

e hold ______ ______ ______

3. Complete these definitions by adding prefixes to the given words and groups of letters.

inter post pre sub super trans contra

a To sink or plunge under the water = ______merge

b An addition to the end of a letter = ______script

c To change the form, character or appearance of something = ______form

d Something that is unnecessary, extra to one's needs = ______fluous

e To break in when someone is speaking = ______rupt

f To argue an opposing point of view = ______dict

g To get ready for something = ______pare

0 Tough OK Got it! 19

Total /19

More practice? Go to www

Lesson 3 Spelling

Number prefixes

The letter strings **uni**, **mono**, **bi**, **tri**, **quad**, **oct** and **dec** are to do with numbers.

bi means two **tri** means three **quad** means four

Knowing these meanings can make it easier to work out the meaning of words that begin with one of these prefixes.

QUICK TIP! You can use a dictionary to check meanings.

1. What are the meanings of these words?

a bicycle ____________ b tricycle ____________

c binoculars ____________ d triple ____________

e biannual ____________ f tricolour ____________

g bilateral ____________ h trilateral ____________

2. Ped means foot in Latin. What do these words mean?

a biped ____________ b triped ____________ c quadruped ____________

3. What do these words mean?

a triangle ____________

b quadrangle ____________

c octagon ____________

d decagon ____________

QUICK TIP! **angulus** = corner in Latin and **gonia** = angle in Greek.

4. Write the meanings of these words.

a decilitre ____________ b octopus ____________

c decimetre ____________ d octet ____________

e decade ____________ f octave ____________

5. Use words beginning with prim (first) or semi (half) in these sentences.

a He lives in the ____________ house across the road.

b The three ____________ colours are red, blue and yellow.

c Half a circle is a ____________.

0 Tough OK Got it! 24

Total /24

More practice? Go to www

Connectives

Connectives connect clauses and sentences together. When two clauses are joined you get two thoughts or actions in the same sentence. Connectives can be:

- short words, like **if**
- made up of two or more words, like **notwithstanding**
- phrases, like **because of**.

1. Underline the connectives in these sentences.

a We had our tea then we played football.

b We did some practice after we tuned our guitars.

c I'd had enough so I went home.

d Coach was cross because I missed a free kick.

2. Match pairs of words together to make connectives and write them on the line.

a where ever ______

b how while ______

c there ever ______

d what over ______

e who fore ______

f mean ever ______

g more as ______

3. Join three words together to make two compound connectives.

never with standing **a** ______

not the less **b** ______

4. Group these connectives according to type.

secondly meanwhile therefore lastly so afterwards

time	**sequence**	**logic**

(6 marks)

0 Tough OK Got it! 19

Total /19

More practice? Go to 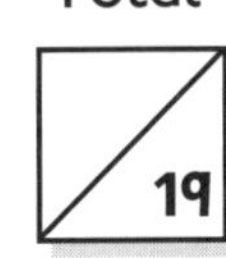

Lesson 5 Spelling

Word origins 1

Over the centuries some words are altered and others are no longer used. Some are shortened or lengthened, others change considerably:

- **sup** has become **supper**
- **methinks** is now **I think**.

1. Join these old-fashioned words to their modern equivalent.

a whither	here	**b** yonder	in truth, in fact
c thither	look at	**d** whence	listen to
e hither	you	**f** thee	over there
g thou	there	**h** verily	from where
i behold	where	**j** hark	you

2. Write the modern equivalent of these words.

a saith	______________	**b** ye	______________
c begone	______________	**d** wherein	______________
e nigh	______________	**f** foe	______________

3. Write these sentences using modern language.

a Whither may I find John?

____

b From that tree yonder may ye see the house.

____

c There will ye find him.

____

d He oftimes cometh hither with his dog.

____

0 Tough OK Got it! 20

Total /20

More practice? Go to www

New words

Spelling | Lesson 6

Inventions, technological developments and new ideas bring words into our language. Sometimes they take the name of the inventor or the process used. For example, **solar power** is a means by which the Sun's rays are converted to generate electricity.

Many new words are used in conversation but tend not to be used in writing until they are very well known.

1. Write the common names used for these inventions and ideas.

a A trade name but commonly used name for a vacuum cleaner. ______________

b A ball-point pen invented by a Hungarian. ______________

c A road surface of crushed small stones and tar developed by J. L. McAdam. ______________

2. Answer these with words that have come into the common English language quite recently.

a A small oven used to cook food quickly using very short electric waves. ______________

b A type of running shoe. ______________

c Riding a bike with the front wheel off the ground. ______________

d A portable computer. ______________

e A car for taking lots of people in. ______________

f A message sent from a computer. ______________

3. New words are often used in conversation before they appear in a dictionary. Write some words (and their definitions!) you use that probably aren't in a dictionary.

Word	Definition
a cool	really great
b	
c	
d	

0 Tough OK Got it! 12

Total /12

More practice? Go to www

Lesson 7 Grammar

Prepositions

Prepositions are words or phrases used before a noun or pronoun to link it to another part of the sentence. They often indicate:

- **direction** (**over** the hill, **up** the stairs)
- **position** (**in** a car, **behind** the door)
- **time** (**during** the film, **on** Monday)

1. Choose a preposition to complete each sentence. Use each preposition once.

during off behind on through under up across in around

a Calvin jumped ________________ the diving board.

b They ran ________________ the road.

c Susan looked ________________ the window.

d They chased each other ________________ the playground.

e The squirrel scrambled ________________ the tree.

f There was a terrific thunderstorm ________________ the night.

g Rosie crawled ________________ her bed looking for her shoe.

h He crept up ________________ his dad and poked him ________________ the ribs.

i The notice went up ________________ the notice board yesterday morning.

QUICK TIP!
Write in pencil so that you can rub a word out if you need to!

2. Select one of the prepositional phrases to complete these sentences.

by means of in accordance with in spite of because of

a She came with us ______________________________ all she had said.

b We got there eventually ______________________________ public transport.

c We set up the experiment ______________________________ the instructions.

d The pavements were icy ______________________________ the steep drop in temperature.

0 Tough	OK	Got it! 13

Total /13

More practice? Go to www

Conventions

Grammar | Lesson 8

In all languages there are rules about the order of words in a sentence, just as there are rules about the letters in a word. There also has to be agreement between the articles, nouns, pronouns, adjectives, verbs and adverbs.

1. Choose the correct article for these phrases: a, an, some.

a _______ trolley **b** _______ orange **c** _______ pears **d** _______ basket

e _______ new shoes **f** _______ object **g** _______ apple **h** _______ road

2. Rearrange and rewrite these phrases so that the adjectives and nouns agree with each other.

a some bike yellow _______________ **b** those six pencil _______________

c a nice houses _______________ **d** an cases empty _______________

e my own beds _______________ **f** the day old good _______________

3. Change the tense of these verbs to agree with the adverbs.

a Ivan saw her tomorrow. _______________

b I will go yesterday. _______________

c Len ran next Sunday. _______________

d Mary will dance last Saturday. _______________

e Ivan played on his Gameboy tomorrow. _______________

4. Rewrite these sentences so that the verb tense and the nouns agree with the rest of the sentence.

a It is fun to went on holiday. _______________

b I like played in the park. _______________

c Bob stays in beds late this morning. _______________

d Tom will trip over a stones yesterday morning. _______________

e Lena will swim in some race last Wednesday. _______________

f A leopard cannot changed his spot. _______________

g You must be homes before sevens o'clock. _______________

h The early bird catched the worms. _______________

0 Tough OK Got it! 27

Total /27

More practice? Go to www

Lesson 9 Grammar

Complex sentences

A complex sentence has a **main clause** and a **subordinate clause**.
A **main clause** makes sense on its own.
A **subordinate clause** does not make sense on its own.

When it started to snow, I went indoors.

subordinate clause — main clause

The subordinate clause adds information to the main clause and starts with a conjunction such as **since**, **when**, **while**, **although**.

1. Underline the main clauses in these sentences and circle the subordinate clauses.

- **a** If we hurry, we will catch the next bus.
- **b** When the bell rang, we went out into the playground.
- **c** He turned off the lights, before he went out.
- **d** To keep the Mongols out of China, the Emperor built the Great Wall.

2. Choose a connective to complete these complex sentences.

after when in case until since because even though although

- **a** ______________ it was time to go, Susie put her coat on.
- **b** Paul listened to some music ______________ she had gone.
- **c** He was enjoying it ______________ his mum yelled at him.
- **d** Linda got up early ______________ she wanted to go for a run.
- **e** Pop took his pullover with him ______________ he felt cold.

3. Turn these sentences round to put the subordinate clause first. Don't forget the punctuation!

- **a** We were woken up when there was a loud hammering on the cabin door.

  ____

- **b** She found it harder and harder to run because of the pelting rain.

  ____

- **c** Father moved back into the crowd once he had helped us into the lifeboats.

  ____

0 Tough OK Got it! 12

Total /12

More practice? Go to www

Active and passive 1

Grammar | Lesson 10

Active sentences tell us that someone (subject) is doing (verb) something (object).
Active means doing something: John **chased** Tim.
Passive sentences tell us that something (object) is being done (verb) to someone (subject).
Passive means letting it happen: Tim **was chased by** John.

1. Write whether these sentences are active or passive.

a Geoff drove Kelly home. ____________

b Kelly was driven home by Geoff. ____________

c Baby Cara was being fed by Mum. ____________

d Mum fed baby Cara. ____________

e Dad is mowing the lawn. ____________

f The lawn is being mowed by Dad. ____________

2. Who was doing what to whom in these active sentences?

	subject	verb	object
a Jane caught the ball.			
b Aaron took some photographs.			
c Jamil rode this bike yesterday.			
d Emily made a chocolate cake.			

3. What was being done by whom in these passive sentences?

	subject	verb	object
a The ball was caught by Jane.			
b Some photographs were taken by Aaron.			
c This bike was ridden by Jamil yesterday.			
d The chocolate cake was made by Emily.			

0 Tough OK Got it! 14

Total /14

More practice? Go to www

Lesson 11 Grammar

Active and passive 2

Active sentences can be changed into passive sentences, and passive sentences can be changed into active sentences.

Passive The ball was hit by Bella.
Active Bella hit the ball.

1. **Change these passive sentences into active sentences.**

   a The school was told about the new building by the head teacher.

   ____

   b The Junior League was won at Denby, North Carolina by Henfield School.

   ____

   c The winning horse was ridden by an unknown jockey.

   ____

   d All the fruit juice had been drunk by the team.

   ____

2. **Change these active sentences into passive ones.**

   a Joe will drive Emma home. ______________________________

   b The dog bit a boy. ______________________________

   c The policeman chased the thief. ______________________________

   d The dog ate the remains of the pie. ______________________________

3. **Instructions are written using active sentences. Imagine you watched someone following these instructions. Write what they did.** *(4 marks)*

   Put a teaspoon of salt into $\frac{1}{4}$ litre of water. Stir the mixture and pour it into a bowl. Place the bowl on the window sill in the sunlight. Leave the dish there until all the water has evaporated and then leave it for a further 24 hours before examining it.

   A teaspoon of salt was put into $\frac{1}{4}$ litre of water. ______________________________

   ____

   ____

   ____

0 Tough	OK	Got it! 12

Total
/12

More practice? Go to www

Colons and semi-colons

Colons are used to introduce lists, quotations and explanations:
He bought: eggs, flour, sugar and milk. His reason was this: the birthday cake.

Semi-colons have several uses. The most common ones are:
- in **complex lists**: He has frogs and bats; snails and mice; pigs and cows.
- to **link sentences** instead of conjunctions: Mice eat cheese; cows eat grass.
- to **precede conjunctions** such as: however, nevertheless, that is to say.

1. Write the missing colons and commas, if required, in these sentences.

a The list of ingredients included chicken onions mushrooms tomatoes and seasoning.

b The characters in the story included Dorothy the lion the scarecrow and the tin man.

c I am away on the following days 3 March 22 April 8 and 15 May.

d Your duties to sweep the stairs and to dust the hall.

2. Write the missing colons in these explanations.

a There was only one thing they could do hide.

b The information had just come through the contract was signed.

c The exam results were on the notice board they had all passed.

3. Write the missing semi-colons in these complex lists.

a She sent cards to Mike in Melbourne Laura in Perth Ravi in California and Heidi in Iowa.

b The chef needed strips of raw chicken thin slices of courgettes some bamboo shoots and oil.

4. Use semi-colons to join the two main clauses in these sentences.

a Some people are good at games some are not.

b A few of us wanted to go to India the rest wanted to go to Thailand.

c She had been brought up in France but they still considered her to be English.

5. Write semi-colons before the conjunctions in these sentences.

a She was encouraged to run every day however, it was not compulsory.

b No one stood over him while he worked nevertheless, he always tried his hardest.

0 Tough OK Got it! 14

Total /14

More practice? Go to www

Lesson 13 Punctuation

Hyphens and dashes

Hyphens can be used:

- to form **compound** words:
  steam-roller
- to clarify the **meaning** of some words:
  He saw a man-eating tiger. (Not a man eating tiger for dinner)
- to **split** the word at the end of a syllable if the whole word cannot be written on one line:
  amuse-
  ment.

Dashes are used to show breaks in sentences in informal writing and for emphasis:
There were five cats on the sofa – and they were all black.

1. Put the missing hyphens into these compound words.

a hanggliding ____________ **b** sisterinlaw ____________

c windowshopping ____________ **d** weightbearing ____________

2. Put the missing hyphens into these sentences.

a The passers by looked at the new poster.

b Peru is a Spanish speaking country.

c The alarm made a high pitched sound.

d The baby sitter arrived at 7.30 pm.

3. Put hyphens into these words to show sensible places to split them if they each had to be split across two lines.

a marvellous ____________ **b** opportunity ____________

4. Use dashes to emphasise a point being made in each of these sentences.

a He had originally thought there was no point in running but he changed his mind!

____

b I'll say it again I don't think you're listening.

____

0 Tough OK Got it! 12

Total /12

More practice? Go to 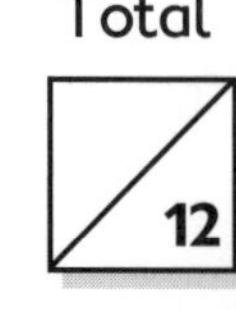

Commas and brackets

Commas are used to add a comment, an aside, in a sentence:

We went to St. Paul's, in London, to see a concert.

Brackets come in pairs and can be used:

- to insert a useful (but not essential) piece of information: Charles Kingsley (1819–75) wrote *The Water Babies*.
- to mark off numerals, alternatives and abbreviations: London Heathrow Airport (LHR).

1. Use commas to separate the aside from the main sentence.

a We went to Winchester in Hampshire to see the cathedral.

b It was on balance a pretty good idea.

c They had arrived at long last in Edinburgh.

d Alan Paton the prize-winning South African novelist wrote *Cry the Beloved Country*.

e Now she thought it is time to leave.

2. Put brackets into these sentences to enclose the non-essential information.

a Michael Foreman born 1938 is a prolific illustrator and author.

b The discoverer of penicillin Alexander Fleming was Scottish.

c Claude Monet's painting *Impression: Sunrise* 1872 gave its name to Impressionism.

d London UK is one of the largest cities in the world.

3. Put brackets round the alternative ways of writing the words.

a Mark claims he saw an Unidentified Flying Object UFO last night.

b The English we are taught in schools is from the National Literacy Strategy NLS.

c The fee is ten pounds £10.

0 Tough OK Got it! 12

Total /12

More practice? Go to www

Lesson 15 Comprehension

Classic fiction

This is a short extract from a **classic novel** by Charles Dickens. It uses a lot of **dialogue** and **colloquial language**.

Read the extract and then answer the questions.

"Hold your noise!" cried a terrible voice, as a man started up from among the graves at the side of the church porch. "Keep still, you little devil, or I'll cut your throat!"

A fearful man, all in coarse grey, with a great iron ring on his leg. A man with no hat, and with broken shoes, and with an old rag tied round his head. A man whose teeth chattered in his head as he seized me by the chin.

"O! Don't cut my throat, sir," I pleaded in terror. "Pray don't do it, sir."

"Tell us your name!" said the man. "Quick!"

"Pip, sir."

"Show us where you live," said the man. "Point out the place!"

I pointed to where our village lay, on the flat in-shore among the alder-trees and pollards, a mile or more from the church.

The man, after looking at me for a moment, turned me upside down, and emptied my pockets. There was nothing in them but a piece of bread.

"You young dog," said the man, licking his lips, "what fat cheeks you ha' got. Where's your mother?"

"There, sir!" said I.

He started, made a short run, and stopped and looked over his shoulder.

"There, sir!" I timidly explained. " 'Also Georgiana'. That's my mother."

"Oh!" said he, coming back. "And is that your father lying alongside your mother?"

"Yes, sir," said I; "him too; 'late of this parish'."

"Ha!" he muttered then, considering. "Who d'ye live with – supposin' you're kindly let to live, which I han't made up my mind about?"

"My sister, sir – Mrs. Joe Gargery – wife of Joe Gargery, the blacksmith, sir."

"Blacksmith, eh?" said he. And looked down at his leg. "Now lookee here," he said, "the question being whether you're to be let to live. You know what a file is? And you know what provisions are?"

"Yes, sir."

"You get me a file." He tilted me upside down. "And you get me food." He tilted me again. "You bring 'em both to me." He tilted me again. "Or I'll have your heart and liver out."

I said that I would get him the file, and I would get him what broken bits of food I could, and I would come to him at the Battery, early in the morning.

"Say Lord strike you dead if you don't!" said the man.

"Goo-good night, sir," I faltered.

Circle the right answer.

1. **The story takes place in:**

a field | a church | a prison | a graveyard

2. **On his leg the prisoner had:**

a boot | a plaster | an iron ring | some grey cloth

3. **Pip's sister is married to:**

a teacher | a farmer | a blacksmith | a prison guard

4. **'Late of this parish' means:**

gone away | now dead | living in the village | always late

5. **Write down six things you know about the prisoner from this passage.** *(6 marks)*

____

____

6. **What two things did the prisoner want? Why was each one so important to him?** *(2 marks)*

____

____

7. **Why did the prisoner start to run when Pip said his mother was 'There, sir'?**

____

____

8. **How did Pip feel during the meeting? Find two sentences that explain this.** *(2 marks)*

____

____

0 Tough | OK | Got it! 15

Total /15

More practice? Go to www

Lesson 16 Comprehension

Non-chronological reports

Non-chronological reports are **information texts** that do not follow a time sequence. Non-fiction books, information leaflets and tourist brochures are all examples of non-chronological reports. They tend to:

- have a clear **introductory paragraph** and a **concluding comment**
- follow a **clear** and **logical order** in the main paragraphs
- offer **facts**, not opinions
- be written in a **formal** style and in the **present** tense (except for historical reports)
- use **connectives** – for example to show comparisons or additional comments
- use precise, **descriptive** and **technical** language.

Read this non-chronological report, then answer the questions.

The Lake District is a popular National Park. More and more people enjoy its fantastic scenery each year, due to increasing numbers of car owners and improvements to local roads and motorways. This, however, is placing an ever-increasing pressure on this beautiful and valuable environment.

Traffic jams in and around the Lake District create air pollution. Parking facilities at most tourist sites are overflowing in peak season, causing visitors to park on grass verges, which in turn causes soil erosion. Litter is also a problem, although many bins are provided and people are encouraged to take their litter home.

Activities such as hiking, camping and mountain biking cause severe footpath erosion. Visitors often leave the designated trails, risking nesting birds and animals being disturbed, vegetation being destroyed and water courses becoming polluted.

In addition, the traditional hill farming of the Lake District has effects on the landscape. Grazing sheep keep the grass short and eat other vegetation, including young saplings. The difficulty faced now is how to preserve the beauty of this area without lowering the enjoyment of visitors or impairing the livelihoods of local farmers.

1. **What is the Lake District?** ______________________________

2. **Give three reasons why so many people come to the Lake District now.**

   a ______________________________

   b ______________________________

   c ______________________________

3. **List six key problems caused by visitor numbers:**

a ______________________________

b ______________________________

c ______________________________

d ______________________________

e ______________________________

f ______________________________

4. **Give four examples of technical vocabulary used in this report.**

a ______________ b ______________

c ______________ d ______________

5. **Circle the connectives used in this report.**

6. **What is the main purpose of this non-chronological report?**

____

____

7. **Which sentence introduces the main focus of this report?**

____

8. **Is the information in the report organised in a logical order? Explain your answer.**

____

____

9. **Does the author express any personal opinions? Explain your answer.**

____

____

0 Tough OK Got it! 19

Total /19

More practice? Go to www

How am I doing?

1. **Underline the unstressed vowels in these words.**

a Wednesday	**b** government	**c** chimney	**d** geography
e cupboard	**f** Saturday	**g** skeleton	**h** raspberry
i parallel	**j** constable	**k** lavatory	**l** library

2. **Underline the root words in these words.**

a classify	**b** artistically	**c** longevity	**d** ageism	**e** magnetise
f childishness	**g** enjoyment	**h** unhappily	**i** impossibility	**j** immobility

3. **Use a word beginning with the given prefix to complete these sentences.**

a They lived in a sub__________ of London.

b She spoke fluent French so she was able to trans__________ the document.

c A teacher was sent to super__________ the children doing the exam.

d We need to post__________ our visit.

4. **What are the meanings of these Latin prefixes?**

a bi __________ **b** tri __________ **c** quad __________ **d** dec __________

5. **Use a word beginning with one of the prefixes above to provide the answers.**

a Something you ride on with two wheels. ____________________

b A four-sided yard. ____________________

c A period of ten years. ____________________

d In geometry – a three-sided shape. ____________________

6. **Choose a connective to complete these sentences.**

whenever but so on the other hand although

a We could go for a walk; ________________, we could go to the shops.

b ________________ she left her old teddy bear, Jan took her new book with her.

c All my family are blond ________________ I am a brunette.

d He kept his kit handy ________________ he could grab it when it was time to leave.

e ________________ you feel like going, just let me know.

7. **Fill in the spaces with one of these prepositions. Use each preposition once.**

across along about inside against through into

a It will be ____________ four o'clock by the time we get there.

b We ran ____________ the pavement and out ____________ the gate.

c Carole was leaning ____________ the gate waiting for me.

d We went __________ the house and __________ the hallway __________ the kitchen.

8. **Rewrite these sentences so that the nouns, adjectives and verbs agree.**

a A stitches in times saved nines. ______________________________

b Playtimes comes after Literacies. ______________________________

c We clap our hand when we see the clowns. ______________________________

d Too many cook spoils the broths. ______________________________

9. **Use conjunctions to complete these sentences.**

a ____________ you can have your pudding, you must eat your main course.

b ____________ it was time to go, we still were not ready.

d ____________ Mum had closed the shop, we couldn't go home.

10. **Change these sentences from active to passive.**

a The pancake had been eaten by Charlie. ______________________________

b The shoelaces of Anna were tied by Mum. ______________________________

c A new hockey stick was bought by Lois. ______________________________

11. **Rewrite these sentences putting in the missing commas, colons or semi-colons.**

a Marc's bag held the following his homework a book two biros a pencil and a rubber.

____

b The house was sold they were finally moving to France.

____

12. **Write the missing hyphens.**

a Eddie was standard bearer at the presentation.

b Montreal is the second largest French speaking city in the world.

c The cries of cock a doodle do filled the air.

Total

/ **58**

More practice? Go to www

Lesson 17 Spelling

Unstressed letters

Spelling words with unstressed letters can be made easier using these suggestions:

1 Break a word down into **syllables** and pronounce each one: personal – per / son / al.
2 Think of **other words** that come from the **same root**: medicine – medic.
3 Look for **words within words**: business – business.

QUICK TIP!
Words can have more than one unstressed letter.

1. Split these words into syllables, then underline the unstressed letters.

a Tuesday ____________ **b** Saturday ____________

c dietary ____________ **d** flavour ____________

e victory ____________ **f** savoury ____________

2. Underline the unstressed letters. Which word or words within the words below could help you remember the unstressed letters?

a mathematics ____________ **b** cupboard ____________

c carpet ____________ **d** portable ____________

3. Rewrite these words correctly, putting in the missing unstressed letters.

a Wensdy ____________ **b** hanbag ____________

c rasbry ____________ **d** enviruhmunt ____________

e extruh ____________ **f** govuhmunt ____________

g compny ____________ **h** poisnus ____________

i jewellry ____________ **j** diffrunt ____________

4. Use one of the words on this page to complete these sentences.

a Mum went out to the shops and left her ____________ behind.

b Deadly nightshade is so called because it is ____________ .

c The ____________ rule our country.

d How many ____________ animals can you see?

0 Tough OK Got it! 24

Total /24

More practice? Go to www

Prefixes

If you can recognise a **prefix** in an unfamiliar word, it can help you to **spell** the word correctly and make it possible for you to **guess** the meaning of the unknown word.

1. Link these prefixes with their meanings.

a audi **b** micro **c** tele **d** duo **e** hydro **f** port **g** prim

distant water hear carry first small two

2. Read the definitions and add the correct prefix to complete each word.

a If an object is easy to carry it is ______able.

b ________logy is the study of water resources in land.

c A ________balance is a balance for measuring very small weights.

d A ______tone is a drawing or painting created in two tones or colours.

3. Complete each of these sets of words with a prefix from question 1.

a ______graph ______phone ______vision ______scope

b ______ence ______torium ______tion ______ble

c ______ary ______ate ______itive ______acy

4. Write one word that you know that begins with each of these prefixes:

a tele ________

b micro ________

c auto ________

d anti ________

e sub ________

f extra ________

g inter ________

h semi ________

0 Tough OK Got it! 22

Total /22

More practice? Go to www

Lesson 19 Spelling

Spelling strategies

Seeing that words belong in families can help with spelling.
If you can spell **probable**, you can easily spell **probably**, **improbable**, **probability**.
If you can spell **care**, you can easily spell **careful**, **careless**, **carelessly**.

1. Use both a prefix and a suffix to make a new word from each of the words below. Choose from the following each time. The first one has been done for you.

Prefixes: ir, im, in, un.

Suffixes: ful, ness, able, ly

a important unimportantly

b religious ____________

c frequent ____________

d kind ____________

e fortunate ____________

f fear ____________

g thought ____________

h accept ____________

2. Make two more family words for each of the following. You may need to change the end of the first word. The first one has been done for you.

a sensitive insensitive sensitivity

b memory ____________ ____________

c accept ____________ ____________

d guilt ____________ ____________

e courage ____________ ____________

f conscious ____________ ____________

g critical ____________ ____________

h relevant ____________ ____________

i meaning ____________ ____________

j friend ____________ ____________

k hostile ____________ ____________

l peace ____________ ____________

0 Tough OK Got it! 18

Total /18

More practice? Go to 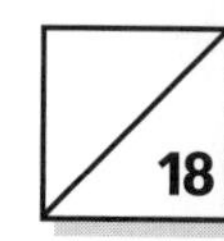

Word origins 2

Spelling Lesson 20

The English language has **evolved** over many years, through the influences of several different languages including Celtic, Latin, Greek, German, Norse and Old French.

Knowing about the **origin** of a word can help us find out its meaning and to learn its spelling.

1. Write the correct Latin prefix to complete each word.

ad circum contra dis ex extra im ob post semi pre

a	______navigate	**b**	______dict	**c**	______mediate	**d**	______terrestrial
e	______pone	**f**	______circular	**g**	______tuse	**h**	______minister
i	______appear	**j**	______terminate	**k**	______pay	**l**	______belief

2. Create nouns using these suffixes, which come from Latin.

-ment, **-ion** = result of an action or process **-acy** = a state of being

a	private __________	**b**	bewilder __________	**c**	reduce __________
d	discuss __________	**e**	harass __________	**f**	accurate __________
g	delicate __________	**h**	process __________	**i**	embarrass __________

3. The English words on the left have been split in two to show the two Greek words from which they are made. Match each pair of Greek words with their meaning on the right.

a	auto-graph	half-globe
b	micro-phone	water-fear
c	hemi-sphere	self-write
d	macro-climate	through-measure
e	hydro-phobia	small-voice
f	dia-meter	large-region

QUICK TIP!
Word origins are given in **etymological** dictionaries.

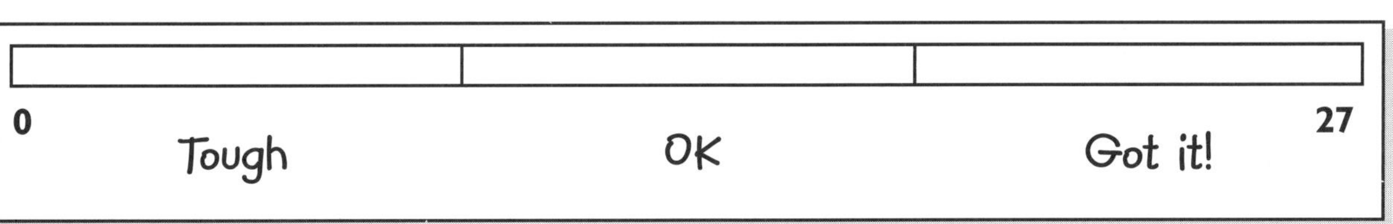

Total
/27

More practice? Go to www

Lesson 21 Spelling

Proverbs

Proverbs are short, memorable **sayings** that express widely held views or contain advice.

'A house is not a home' means that a house is just a building; it is the family inside that makes it a home.

1. Tick the proverbs and put a cross next to sentences that are not proverbs.

a A change is as good as a rest. ___

b The Sun is shining brightly in the sky. ___

c Make hay while the Sun shines. ___

d A fool and his money are soon parted. ___

e A leopard cannot change his spots. ___

f Actions speak louder than words. ___

2. Join the two halves of these proverbs.

a Every cloud	gathers no moss.
b A little of what you fancy	is a friend indeed.
c A rolling stone	has a silver lining.
d A friend in need	does you good.

3. Match these proverbs to their meanings.

a Many hands make light work.	Things can be ruined if lots of people are involved.
b Too many cooks spoil the broth.	It's best to leave things as they are.
c Let sleeping dogs lie.	Jobs are easier when many people do them.

4. What do you think these proverbs mean?

a A stitch in time saves nine.

___

b Don't cry over spilt milk.

___

c Don't count your chickens until they're hatched.

___

0 Tough OK Got it! 16

Total /16

More practice? Go to 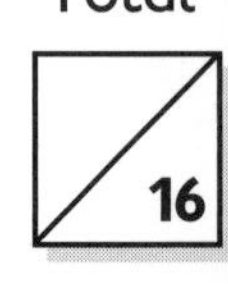

Structuring arguments

An **argument** is a **fact** or **statement** that is put forward to support an **opinion** during a discussion or debate on a particular topic. Arguments can be **for** or **against** the proposal or idea being discussed.

Connectives such as **similarly**, **but** and **despite the fact that** help to structure arguments.

1. Write in the connectives to link both sides of these arguments.

although on the other hand alternatively on the one hand

a I couldn't decide what to do. ________________ I needed to go shopping, ________________ I had a lot of work to finish at home.

b He is a good rugby player, ___________ you'd never think so to look at him.

c We could start a new design from scratch. ____________, we could use the same drawing and just amend it slightly.

2. Underline the connectives that help to structure the points of this argument.

We would like to argue for the construction of a new school dining room.

Whereas many schools have separate dining rooms, our school currently uses classroom J4 as the dining room. This classroom is too small for all children to sit comfortably and eat lunch at the same time so, in order to avoid overcrowding, a rota has had to be designed for lunch groups. As a result, not all children enjoy their full lunchtime in the playground and are not getting enough exercise.

Furthermore, we have our afternoon lessons in classroom J4 and we always have to wipe down the desks and chairs before we can start work. What's more, even though the windows are open, the room usually smells of stale food.

We understand that the school governors are considering re-turfing the football pitch; however, we think that the money would benefit more children if it were put towards the development of a new school dining room. *(7 marks)*

0 Tough OK Got it! 10

Total /10

More practice? Go to www

Lesson 23 Grammar

Active and passive 3

Sentences are usually written in the **active voice** – showing that the subject **performs** the action.

I sold the house.

Passive sentences are used when it is more important to **emphasise the action** that is being done or **the person or thing it is done to**, rather than who is performing the action.

The house **was sold**.

1. Underline the verbs in these sentences and say whether they are active or passive.

- **a** Sue signed all the letters. ____________
- **b** The room was cluttered with books and papers. ____________
- **c** Mike invited Shereen to go to a party. ____________
- **d** Ali was sitting on a bench with Conrad. ____________
- **e** They had been warned by their father to keep away from next door's dog. ____________

2. Change these sentences from active to passive ones. The first one is done for you.

- **a** Dad kept all his tools in the shed. All Dad's tools were kept in the shed.
- **b** Robin propped his bike against the fence. ____________
- **c** Mum's shopping filled six bags. ____________
- **d** Jill tidied the notice board. ____________
- **e** Grandpa swept the front path. ____________

3. Turn these passive sentences into active ones, removing any unnecessary words.

- **a** The drums were being played by Mick, and the cymbals were being played by Lisa.

  ____
- **b** The shirt bought by Sara was a pink one, and the shirt bought by Claire was a blue one.

  ____
- **c** It was when the window cleaner's ladder fell over that Ruth was struck on the head.

  ____
- **d** They were told by Dr Barnett to take Raj to hospital.

  ____

0 Tough OK Got it! 14

Total

/14

More practice? Go to www

Formal language

Formal language is used for instructions, commands, reports, explanatory text and official letters. It is written in an **impersonal style** – the author's voice is not heard and a specific reader is not identified.

Passive sentences and **imperative verbs** – ones giving orders or commands – are often used:

Smoking is not allowed. Keep to the left.

1. Match the formal and informal styles of these notices.

Formal	Informal
a Keep off the grass.	Sorry, but we have to charge for all breakages.
b Parking is for permit holders only.	Please don't walk on our grass.
c Breakages must be paid for.	You can't park here without a permit.

2. Rewrite these requests in a formal style, using imperative verbs forms.

a We would like you all to park on the left.

____

b You can't bring children in here.

____

c Please don't talk in the corridor, children.

____

3. Rewrite this note using formal language. *(4 marks)*

QUICK TIP!
The date is always given on formal letters.

Hi Sarah!

In case you don't know, your electricity is going off later, probably around 10am. Should be back on at about 4pm.

Cheers!

The electricity guy

Dear Ms Jones ______________________________

____

____

____

0 Tough OK Got it! 10

Total /10

Lesson 25 Grammar

Complex sentences

In complex sentences the main and subordinate clauses are joined by a **subordinating conjunction** or phrase, such as:

until even though after since although

The subordinate clause can be placed **before**, **within** or **after** the main clause, but must be introduced by a conjunction:

She wanted to go, **if** it were possible, to the theme park.

1. Circle the conjunctions and underline the subordinate clauses below.

a Before you sit down to dinner, go and wash your hands.

b After pitching our tents, we started to climb the hill.

c That taller boy, who was wearing a green tracksuit, turned to face me.

d The London Marathon, which is run by people of all ages, is 26 miles long.

2. What separates the clauses in the sentences above? ____________________

3. Choose a suitable subordinating conjunction to complete these sentences

a Give him some, __________ not all, of the foreign coins.

b __________ it was a warm day, Nick stayed indoors.

c She had an itch, __________ was in the middle of her back, and she couldn't reach it.

d __________ their late departure, they arrived before the rest of the group.

e __________ the postman comes, I will have to wait in the flat.

f __________ the match, they had tea with the other team.

g It took two hours to get there, __________ the traffic jam.

0 Tough OK Got it! 12

Total /12

More practice? Go to www

No Nonsense
English

10–11
years

Parents' notes

What your child will learn from this book

Bond No Nonsense will help your child to understand and become more confident at English. This book features the main English objectives covered by your child's class teacher during the school year. It provides clear, straightforward teaching and learning of the essentials in a rigorous, step-by-step way.

This book begins with some **handwriting practice**. Encourage your child to complete this carefully and to continue writing neatly throughout the book.

The four types of lessons provided are:
Spelling – these cover spelling rules and strategies.
Grammar – these cover word types and sentence construction.
Punctuation – these cover punctuation marks and their rules.
Comprehension – these cover reading different types of text and comprehension questions.

How you can help

Following a few simple guidelines will ensure that your child gets the best from this book:

- Explain that the book will help your child become confident in their English work.
- If your child has difficulty reading the text on the page or understanding a question, do provide help.
- Encourage your child to complete all the exercises in a lesson. You can mark the work using this answer section (which you will also find on the website). Your child can record their own impressions of the work using the 'How did I do' feature.

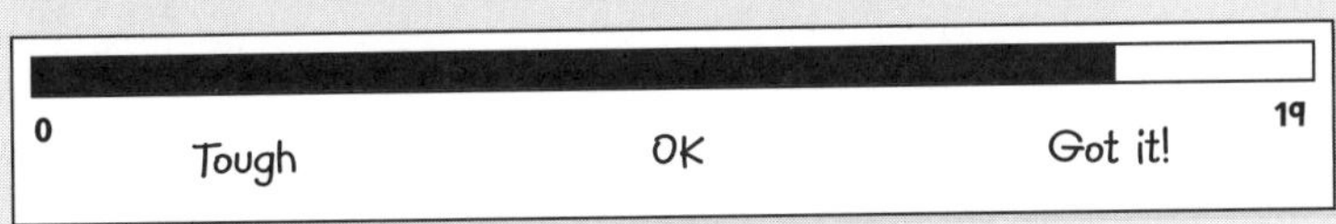

- The 'How am I doing?' sections provide a further review of progress.

Using the website – www.bondlearning.co.uk

- The website provides extra practice of every skill in the book. So if your child does not feel confident about a lesson, they can go to the website and have another go.
- For every page of this book you will find further practice questions and their answers available to download.
- To access the extra practice pages:
  1. Go to www.bondlearning.co.uk
  2. Click on 'English'
  3. Click on '10–11 Years'
  4. Click on the lesson you want.

Bond No Nonsense 10–11 years Answers

1 Unstressed vowels p4

1 a fattening b dandelion c miniature d interest e astronomy
f abandon g lettuce h benefit i journalist j mathematics
2 a television b parliament c alcohol d consonant e describe
f locomotive g signature h medicine i similar j grammar
3 a separate b definite c interesting d telephone e vegetable
f secretary g holiday h conference i lemonade
4 February, January, boundary, stationary, voluntary, veterinary
lottery, stationery, jewellery, battery
history, factory, category

2 Word roots p5

1 a digest b cipher c prefer d hyphen
e valid f integrate g concept h learn
2 Possible answers include:
a artwork, workout, worker b sideways, outside, beside
c sometimes, somewhere, someone d postage, postpone, compost
e behold, holdall, upholds
3 a submerge b postscript c transform d superfluous
e interrupt f contradict g prepare

3 Number prefixes p6

1 a a vehicle with two wheels b a vehicle with three wheels
c a telescope suitable for use with two eyes d threefold/three times as much/to treble
e two-yearly / twice a year f three-coloured
g two-sided h three-sided
2 a an animal with two feet b an object with three feet
c an animal with four feet
3 a a shape with three sides b a shape with four sides
c a shape with eight sides d a shape with ten sides
4 a decilitre: a tenth part of a litre b octopus: a sea creature with eight arms
c decimetre: a tenth of a metre d octet: a group of eight
e decade: ten years
f octave: a note or sound an eighth above or below another
5 a semi-detached b primary c semi-circle

4 Connectives p7

1 a then b after c so d because
2 a whereas b however c therefore d whatever
e whoever f meanwhile g moreover
3 a nevertheless b notwithstanding
4 time: meanwhile / afterwards
sequence: secondly / lastly
logic: therefore / so

5 Word origins 1 p8

1 a whither / where b yonder / over there
c thither / there d whence / from where
e hither / here f thee / you
g thou / you h verily / in truth, in fact
i behold / look at j hark / listen to
2 a say b the/you c go d in what e near f enemy
3 a Where may I find John?
b From that tree over there you can see the house.
c You will find him there.
d He often comes here with his dog.

6 New words p9

1 a Hoover b Biro c Tarmac
2 a microwave b trainers c wheelie
d laptop e people carrier f email
3 Possible answers include:
a cool: neither warm nor cold / trendy
b hip; where the leg joins the pelvis / trendy
c sorted: arranged / done
d wicked: evil or bad person / brilliant

7 Prepositions p10

1 a off b across c through d around e up
f during g under h behind/in i on
2 a in spite of b by means of c in accordance with d because of

8 Conventions p11

1 a a trolley b an orange c some pears d a basket
e some new shoes f an object g an apple h a road
2 a some yellow bikes b those six pencils
c a nice house d an empty case
e my own bed f the good old days
3 a Ivan will see her tomorrow. b I went yesterday.
c Len will run next Sunday. d Mary danced last Saturday.
e Ivan will play on his Gameboy tomorrow.
4 a It is fun to go on holiday. b I like playing in the park.
c Bob stayed in bed late this morning. d Tom tripped over a stone yesterday morning.
e Lena swam in some races last Wednesday.
f A leopard cannot change his spots.
g You must be home before seven o'clock.
h The early bird catches the worm.

9 Complex sentences p12

1 a (If we hurry,) we will catch the next bus.
b (When the bell rang,) we went out into the playground.
c He turned off the lights, (before he went out.)
d (To keep the Mongols out of China,) the Emperor built the Great Wall.
2 a Since / Because / When b after c until / even though
d because e in case
3 a When there was a loud hammering on the cabin door, we were woken up.
b Because of the pelting rain, she found it harder and harder to run.
c Once he had helped us into the lifeboats, Father moved back into the crowd.

10 Active and passive 1 p13

1 a active b passive c passive d active e active f passive
2 a Jane (s) caught (v) ball (o)
b Aaron (s) took (v) photographs (o)
c Jamil (s) rode (v) bike (o)
d Emily (s) made (v) chocolate cake (o)
3 a Jane (s) was caught (v) ball (o)
b Aaron (s) were taken (v) photographs (o)
c Jamil (s) was ridden (v) bike (o)
d Emily (s) was made (v) chocolate cake (o)

11 Active and passive 2 p14

1 a The head teacher told the school about the new building.
b Henfield School won the Junior League at Denby, North Carolina.
c An unknown jockey rode the winning horse.
d The team drank all the fruit juice.
2 a Emma will be driven home by Joe.
b A boy was bitten by the dog.
c The thief was chased by the policeman.
d The remains of the pie were eaten by the dog.
3 A teaspoon of salt was put into $\frac{1}{4}$ litre of water. The mixture was stirred and poured into a bowl. The bowl was placed on the window sill in the sunlight. The dish was left there until all the water had evaporated and left for a further 24 hours before the dish was examined.

12 Colons and semi-colons p15

1 a The list of ingredients included: chicken, onions, mushrooms, tomatoes and seasoning.
b The characters in the story included: Dorothy, the lion, the scarecrow and the tin man.
c I am away on the following days: 3 March, 22 April, 8 and 15 May.
d Your duties: to sweep the stairs and to dust the hall.
2 a There was only one thing they could do: hide.
b The information had just come through: the contract was signed.
c The exam results were on the notice board: they had all passed.
3 a She sent cards to Mike in Melbourne; Laura in Perth; Ravi in California and Heidi in Iowa.
b The chef needed: strips of raw chicken; thin slices of courgettes; some bamboo shoots and oil.
4 a Some people are good at games; some are not.
b A few of us wanted to go to India; the rest wanted to go to Thailand.
c She had been brought up in France; but they still considered her to be English.
5 a She was encouraged to run every day; however, it was not compulsory.
b No one stood over him while he worked; nevertheless, he always tried his hardest.

13 Hyphens and dashes p16

1 a hang-gliding b sister-in-law c window-shopping d weight-bearing
2 a passers-by b Spanish-speaking c high-pitched d baby-sitter
3 a marvel-lous b oppor-tunity
4 a He had originally thought there was no point in running – but he changed his mind!
b I'll say it again – I don't think you're listening.

14 Commas and brackets p17

1 a We went to Winchester, in Hampshire, to see ...
b It was, on balance, a ...
c They had arrived, at long last, ...
d Alan Paton, the prize-winning South African novelist, wrote ...
e Now, she thought, it ...
2 a Michael Foreman (born 1938) is ...
b The discoverer of penicillin (Alexander Fleming) was ...
c Claude Monet's painting *Impression: Sunrise* (1872) gave...
d London (UK) is ...
3 a Mark claims he saw an Unidentified Flying Object (UFO) last night.
b The English we are taught in schools is from the National Literacy Strategy (NLS).
c The fee is ten pounds (£10).

15 Classic fiction p18

1 a graveyard
2 an iron ring
3 a blacksmith
4 now dead
5 Any six of the following: he was a fearful man / he wore coarse grey / he had an iron ring on his leg / he had no hat / he had broken shoes / his teeth chattered / he was cold / he was hungry.
6 Some food because he was very hungry / a file to get the iron ring off his leg.
7 The prisoner thought that Pip's mother was nearby and would catch him.
8 Pip was terrified. Phrases such as the following explain this: "O! Don't cut my throat, sir!" I pleaded in terror. / "There, sir!" I timidly explained. / "Goo-good night, sir," I faltered.

16 Non-chronological reports p20

1 A National Park
2 a It has fantastic scenery.
b There is an increasing number of car owners.
c There have been improvements to local roads and motorways.
3 Possible answers include:
air pollution caused by traffic jams / overflowing car parks / soil erosion caused by parking in verges / litter / footpath erosion caused by outdoor activities / risk to birds and animals because visitors leave paths / pollution of water courses / grazing sheep eat young saplings.
4 Any four from: air pollution / soil erosion / designated trails / vegetation / water courses.
5 due to / however / also / although / In addition
6 The main purpose of this report is to highlight the damaging effect visitors and local farm life are having on the environment in the Lake District.
7 The last sentence of the first paragraph: 'This, however, is placing an ever-increasing pressure on this beautiful and valuable environment.'
8 Yes, the information is presented in a logical order. The first paragraph introduces the topic. The following paragraphs explore the issues in more detail, drawing to a close in the concluding statement of fact.
9 No, the author does not express any personal opinions. This is a non-chronological report which lists the facts of the situation without introducing the voice of the author.

How am I doing?

1 a Wednesday b government c chimney d geography
e cupboard f Saturday g skeleton h raspberry
i parallel j constable k lavatory l library

2 a classify b artistically c longevity d ageism
e magnetise f childishness g enjoyment h unhappily
i impossibility j immobility
3 a suburb b translate c supervise d postpone
4 a two b three c four d ten
5 a bicycle b quadrangle c decade d triangle
6 a on the other hand b Although c but d so
e Whenever
7 a about b along / through c against d inside / across / into
8 a A stitch in time saves nine.
b Playtime comes after Literacy.
c We clapped our hands when we saw the clowns.
d Too many cooks spoil the broth.
9 a Before b Although c Until
10 a Charlie had eaten the pancake. b Mum tied Anna's shoelaces.
c Lois bought a new hockey stick.
11 a Marc's bag held the following: his homework; a book; two biros; a pencil and a rubber.
b The house was sold; they were finally moving to France.
12 a Eddie was standard-bearer at the presentation
b Montreal is the second largest French-speaking city in the world.
c The cries of cock-a-doodle-do filled the air.

17 Unstressed letters p24

1 a Tues / day b Sat / ur / day c di / et / a / ry d fla / vour
e vic / tor / y f sav / our / y
2 a mathematics: the, he, hem, them b cupboard: cup, up / board, boar, oar
c carpet: pet d portable: tab, table, able
3 a Wednesday b handbag c raspberry d environment
e extra f government g company h poisonous
i jewellery j different
4 a handbag b poisonous c government d different

18 Prefixes p25

1 a audi / hear b micro / small c tele / distant d duo / two
e hydro / water f port / carry g prim / first
2 a portable b Hydrology c microbalance d duotone
3 a tele b audi c prim
4 Possible answers include:
a telephone b microphone c autograph d anticlockwise
e submarine f extraterrestrial g international h semicircular

19 Spelling strategies p26

1 b irreligiously c infrequently d unkindly / unkindness
e unfortunately f unfearful g unthoughtful
h unacceptable
2 Possible answers include:
b memorable / unmemorable / memorably c acceptance / unacceptable / unacceptably
d guilty / guiltless / guiltily e encouragement / courageous
f consciously / unconscious / consciousness g criticism / critically / uncritical
h irrelevant / relevantly / relevance i meaningless / meaningful / meaningfully
j friendless / friendly / unfriendly k hostility / unhostile
l peaceful / peacefully

20 Word origins 2 p27

1 a circumnavigate b contradict c immediate
d extraterrestrial e postpone f semicircular
g obtuse h administer i disappear
j exterminate k prepay l disbelief
2 a privacy b bewilderment c reduction
d discussion e harassment f accuracy
g delicacy h procession i embarrassment
3 a autograph: self-write b microphone: small-voice
c hemisphere: half-globe d macroclimate: large-region
e hydrophobia: water-fear f diameter: through-measure

21 Proverbs p28

1 a ✓ b ✗ c ✓ d ✓ e ✓ f ✓
2 a Every cloud has a silver lining.
b A little of what you fancy does you good.
c A rolling stone gathers no moss.
d A friend in need is a friend indeed.
3 a Many hands make light work. / Jobs are easier when many people do them.
b Too many cooks spoil the broth. / Things can be ruined if lots of people are involved.
c Let sleeping dogs lie. / It's best to leave things as they are.
4 a If you do a simple task at the right time, it could save you severe problems later on.
b There is no point worrying about something which has already happened and cannot be changed.
c Don't assume something until it has actually happened.

22 Structuring arguments p29

1 a On the one hand / On the other hand
b although
c Alternatively
2 Whereas / so, in order to / As a result / Furthermore / What's more / even though / however

23 Active and passive 3 p30

1 a signed / active b was cluttered / passive c invited / active
d was sitting / active e had been warned / passive
2 b The bike was propped against the fence by Robin.
c Six bags were filled with Mum's shopping.
d The notice board was tidied by Jill.
e The front path was swept by Grandpa.
3 a Mick played the drums and Lisa (played) the cymbals.
b Sara bought a pink shirt and Claire (bought) a blue one.
c The window cleaner's ladder struck Ruth on the head when it fell over.
d Dr Barnett told them to take Raj to hospital.

24 Formal language p31

1 a Keep off the grass. / Please don't walk on our grass.
b Parking for permit holders only. / You can't park here without a permit.
c Breakages must be paid for. / Sorry, but we have to charge for all breakages.
2 Possible answers include:
a Park on the left.
b Children may not be brought inside.
c Children are not allowed to talk in the corridor.
3 Possible answers include:
Dear Ms Jones
You may be unaware that from 10am this morning, your electricity will be temporarily disconnected. Your supply should be reconnected by approximately 4pm this afternoon.
We apologise for any inconvenience this may cause.
Yours sincerely,
Southern Electricity Board

25 Complex sentences p32

1 a conjunction: Before / subordinate clause: Before you sit down to dinner
b conjunction: After / subordinate clause: After pitching our tents
c conjunction: who / subordinate clause: who was wearing a green tracksuit.
d conjunction: which / subordinate clause: which is run by people of all ages
2 commas
3 a but / if b Although c which d Despite
e Until f After g because of

26 Contracting sentences p33

1 a Lots of ~~sticky brown~~ chocolate was smeared all over her ~~chubby round~~ cheeks.
b With long ~~extended~~ strides, the ~~spotted~~ cheetah raced after the ~~small young~~ zebra.
c The ~~enormous black~~ bear ~~gently~~ held the ~~little tiny~~ cub in its ~~large padded~~ paw.
2 First it is important to shut gates. Never pick plants. Dogs should be kept on leads. Walk carefully to avoid disturbance to wildlife.
3 Possible answers include:
Garbles: brown, hole-dwelling. Food: zat weed, bongo grass, nocturnal, feeds in Darfar swamps. Adult 2m, ivory tusks, long ears. Babies born blind, see after 2wks. Enemy: rocky eagle – wingspan 3m, nest Harfar mountains, night vision.

27 Conditionals p34

1 a If / then b provided that c on condition that
d would / if e would / if / could f could / provided that
2 a If this were a magic carpet I could fly away.
b Provided that you finish your homework you can go to Terry's.
c If you are not careful you could fall and break your leg.
d Unless I tidy my room I cannot go to the cinema.

28 Apostrophes p35

1 a It's no use, I can't sleep. b You should've said. I could've helped.
c They mustn't go, I haven't said goodbye. d "That's strange! Where's Tom?"
e Who's got a torch? It's dark in here!
2 a Sophie's book. b The fox's tail.
c The chair's leg. d Ranjit and Stuart's project.
3 couldn't / Mum's / 3 o'clock / Grandpa's / Mum's / could've / We'd /Jones' / Grandpa's / sister's

29 Dialogue p36

1 a "Look!" the boy shouted. "Look up there!"
b "Come here, Tom," demanded Dad, "and sort your room out!"
c "Stop!" bellowed the policeman. "Stop at once!"
d "Where on earth did I put my keys?" muttered Mum.
2 "Mum?" called Juhi.
"Yes," replied Mum. "What's the matter?"
"I can't find my school bag. I have looked in my bedroom, in your room and in Raj's room but it doesn't seem to be here. Can you see it downstairs anywhere?"
"I haven't noticed it down here," said Mum, "but I'll have a look for you."
"Thanks Mum. You're the best!" shouted Juhi.

30 Commas p37

1 a Mr Reeves handed out pens, rulers, individual whiteboards and cloths to the class.
b Despite the fact that she had a cold, she was prepared to sing in the choir.
c Meanwhile, back stage, tension was mounting.
d Hans Christian Anderson, the Danish writer, is famous for his fairy tales.
e I wanted a bike, a computer game, some books and a pair of shoes for my birthday.
f William I, known as William the Conqueror, invaded England in 1066.
2 a Outside, the playground was empty.
b I want you to go with Mary, Jamil.
c Michael and James, the Petersen twins, are rowing.
d For afternoon tea, cakes and rolls were served.
3 a My uncle Ted is a teacher. / Ted is one of my uncles.
b My uncle, Ted, is a teacher. / My only uncle, Ted, is a teacher.
c Animals which are dangerous are to be avoided./ Some animals are dangerous.
d Animals, which are dangerous, are to be avoided. / All animals are dangerous.

31 Nonsense poetry p38

1 He was lonely: very few people come by.
2 Possible answers include:
The hat is made of beaver skin. It is 102 feet wide. It is decorated with ribbons and bibbons and bells, buttons, loops and lace.
3 The Quangle Wangle, the Fimble Fowl, the Golden Grouse, the Pobble, the Dong, the Blue Babboon, the Orient Calf, the Attery squash, the Bisky Bat.
4 It was a 'spot so charmingly airy'.
5 bells and buttons / loops and lace / Jam and Jelly / Fimble Fowl / Bumble-Bee / Golden Grouse / Blue Babboon / Bisky Bat / Mulberry moon
6 ribbons and bibbons
7 happy and bouncy
8 Answers might include: the enjoyment of the nonsense words, the rhythm and rhyme of the poem, the strangeness of the creatures, the vividness of the descriptions.

32 Balanced arguments p40

1 The first fact states that most children in the UK wear uniform.
2 as / and that / On the other hand / and / because / While / However / while
3 Some people believe / Considerable debate has taken place / Supporters of school uniform believe / They state / many people would argue
4 normal clothes **might** be / clothing **could** take / people **would** argue / and **would** support / asking **if** anyone / pupils **might** dislike / schools **should** have / it **might** now
5 School uniform helps provide a positive way of reducing discipline problems; it increases school safety; school uniform does not distract a pupil's attention away from their studies.
6 Children are more interested in labels than in school work.
7 Normal clothes do not distract a pupil's attention from their studies.
8 The argument suggests those against school uniform could provide proof by asking children if they have ever been distracted from work by someone's shirt being too bright.
9 Yes, the writer includes a qualified personal opinion in the last sentence, introducing his/her view by stating: 'it is this writer's view that'.
10 Possible answers include:
Yes, because it gives arguments for and against wearing school uniform before drawing a conclusion on the evidence presented.

How am I doing?

1 **a** generally **b** generous **c** marriage **d** handkerchief **e** memorable
2 Possible answers include:
a automobile /autograph / autobiography /automatic
b television / telephone / telescope
c submarine / submerge / subject
3 **a** microphone **b** telegram **c** audience
4 **a** around **b** half **c** small
5 **a** A bad workman always blames his tools. **b** A fool and his money are soon parted.
c A penny saved is a penny gained. **d** Everything must have a beginning.
e More haste less speed.
6 **a** The window was broken by Mike. **b** The Maths homework was completed.
c The crayons were placed on the table by Ranjna.
7 **a** No dogs allowed. **b** No parking. **c** Don't do that!
8 **a** "Before you sit down, can you pass me my cup of tea?"
b He went to the concert, even though he had a headache.
c While he was in Rome, he went to see an opera.
9 **a** The ~~cheerful, friendly~~ waiter brought ~~four~~ bowls of ~~delicious rosy red~~ raspberries.
b The ~~long-limbed~~ giraffe stood next to his ~~small, stumpy~~ baby by the ~~narrow~~ stream.
c He put the ~~heavy red~~ book and ~~bright blue~~ folder on the ~~large maple coffee~~ table.
10 **a** If / would **b** could / if **c** could / provided that
11 **a** isn't / Dad's / Mum's **b** Sally's / Jess' **c** can't / Raj's / won't / We'll
12 **a** "Let's go to the park," Steve called over the fence to Roger. "Ted's there already."
b "Gran, can we make some angel cakes" asked Bella, "for Mum's birthday?"
c "Look at this mess!" bellowed Mr Jones. "Did you really need to do all this?"

33 Spelling rules 1 p44

1 **a** Drop the e and add the suffix.
b riper **c** nicer **d** ruder **e** closer **f** whiter
2 **a** Double the last letter then add the suffix.
b planning **c** letting **d** knitting **e** shopping **f** drumming
3 **a** Change the y to i and then add the suffix.
b chilliest **c** tiniest **d** easiest **e** happiest **f** funniest
4 **a** careful / careless / carefully **b** pitiful / pitiless / pitifully
c painful / painless / painfully

34 Spelling rules 2 p45

1 **a** Change the y to an i and add es.
b berries **c** families **d** puppies **e** sties **f** parties
2 **a** Change the f to v and add es.
b knives **c** loaves **d** thieves **e** lives **f** shelves
3 **a** mischief **b** ✓ **c** neighbour **d** friend **e** height
f ceiling **g** ✓ **h** ✓ **i** ✓

35 Mnemonics p46

1 **a** beauty **b** benefit **c** rhythm **d** because
2 **a** island **b** busy **c** psalm **d** separate
3 Answers will vary.

36 Inventing words p47

1 **a** sound **b** study **c** writing **d** to yield / give way
e self **f** excessive / superior **g** two **h** abnormal fear
i light **j** air **k** water **l** to record
2 **a** superphone / excessive sound **b** photology / the study of light
c autophobia / a fear of one's self **d** microcede / to give way slightly
e biscope / looks in two directions **f** aquagram / a record of water
g aerography / writing about the air **h** autology / the study of oneself
3 **a** small person **b** water biscuit
c two faces / two sides **d** eight sounds
e self-cleaning **f** fear of the number three or things with three elements
4 Answers will vary.

37 Similes p48

1 **a** mule **b** arrow **c** drowned rat **d** weather **e** ABC
2 as quick as a flash / as happy as larks / stacked like building blocks / as brown as berries / as pleased as punch
3 Possible answers include:
a as quiet as a whisper **b** as tough as gristle
c as bright as the sky **d** as strong as a caveman
e run like a gazelle **f** as thick as glue
4 Possible answers include:
a It was as cheap as chips **b** The plant was as dead as a dodo
c It was as smooth as silk **d** His brain was as sharp as a razor
e Her feet were as warm as coals **f** He was as sly as a fox

38 Metaphors p49

1 **a** is a tip **b** were pools of chocolate **c** traffic was murder
d a heart of stone **e** is a small wilderness
2 **a** green carpet **b** red-handed **c** ball of flames
d little monkey **e** thorny
3 Possible answers include:
a The snow is soft balls of cotton wool **b** Grandpa said that life is a box of treats
c The Sun is a ring of fire **d** Love is a cuddle on a cold night

39 Narrative texts p50

1 **a** false **b** false **c** false **d** false **e** false **f** true
2 Trudy was swimming when Jason bombed her. He had leapt off the side, tucked up his knees, wrapped his arms round them and landed in the pool with an almighty splash – right on top of her. It forced her under the water. She was coughing and choking.
"Somebody help me!"
Somebody did. Hands reached out, pulled her to the surface and helped her out of the pool – Jason's.
"I'm sorry Trudy. I didn't see you there. I was just larking about."
"Well, next time, look first. You could have hurt me, I could have drowned," she shouted, half in anger, half in fright.

40 Instructional texts 1 p51

1 numbered points / diagrams / step-by-step details
2 **a** true **b** false **c** false **d** true **e** true **f** false
g false
3 Possible answers include:
- Go to the library.
- The dictionary section is at the far end on the left.
- There is a SAWF (a synonym, antonym and word finder) on the second shelf
- Look up the word you need.
- Make a note of suitable synonyms.
- Look up synonyms of these words to check if they are more suitable.

41 Persuasive texts p52

1 opinion / powerful adjectives / powerful verbs
2 **a** false **b** true **c** true **d** false **e** false **f** true
g true **h** true **i** false
3 b /c / e

42 Impersonal writing p53

1 a / d / e
2 Fill the kettle with water and switch it on. Cut the jelly into cubes and place it in a measuring jug. Allow the kettle to almost boil, then pour water on the jelly to the 500 ml mark. Stir until the jelly is dissolved. Leave until the jug is cool enough to touch. Pour the jelly into a dish and leave in a cool place until cold. Put in the fridge to set.

43 Paragraphs p54

1 **a** It is the start of the story.
b It introduces a new speaker.
c It introduces a new idea.
2 Jenny slumped down in her seat. Why did boys always have the luck? Why couldn't girls have some too? Her mind was running round in circles.
"Go on then, Jenny love." Her father's voice broke into her thoughts.
"What is it?"
"It's the girls' turn now. You do want a ride on that elephant, don't you?"

44 Formal letters p55

1 a / c / e They all start with a capital letter and are followed by a comma.
2 a / d / e They all start with a capital letter and are followed by a comma.
3 **a** false **b** false
c false (capital letters are used) **d** false
e true **f** false (paragraphs are indented in hand-written formal letters)
4 Answers will vary.

45 Playscripts p56

1 Possible answers include:
The scene is at night. Two beds. A boy's bedroom with posters and clothes scattered around. A light is on. One boy is awake. The other is asleep. The curtains are drawn.
2 Answers will vary.

46 Instructional texts 2 p57

1 Answers will vary.
2 Answers will vary, but ensure the language is formal: You are invited to a party on…
3 The instructions should be written in an impersonal style, using imperatives and should follow a clear, logical and sequential order.
4 Answers will vary.

47 Comparing poems p58

1 A is a rhyming poem, B is blank verse.
2 The sea.
3 **a** A / strength **b** B / weakness **c** B / strength **d** A / weakness
4 Possible answers include:
Poem A evokes a feeling of longing from the reader – it makes the reader want to run away to sea. It creates a sense of freedom.
Poem B evokes a warm, happy feeling and takes the reader back to their own childhood memories – it is likely that everyone has experienced running into the sea when they were younger.
5 Possible answers include:
Poem A includes many descriptive phrases which create vivid pictures of what it is like to sail on the open sea. The rhythm of the poem is bouncy, and the idea that it gives of freedom and excitement is very appealing.
Poem B takes the reader back to their own memories of holidays playing in the sea. It describes a common experience of which most readers will have knowledge and makes it easy for the reader to picture what the poet is remembering. The familiar language of the poem will appeal to most readers.
6 Answers will vary.

48 Skimming and scanning p60

1 The life and work of Michael Foreman.
2 **a** No – the background section looks very brief
b No – the background section looks very brief
c Yes – the heading of the second section is 'Career'
3 The heading of the third is 'Inspirational sources' and sounds more interesting than 'Background' or 'Career'.
4 He is an author and one of the world's leading illustrators of children's books.
5 Born in Pakefield, Suffolk – 1938.
6 He has designed TV commericals and Christmas stamps.
7 Over 100 books
8 He has written 30 books.
9 He has won many prizes – the Kate Greenaway Award, for example.
10 He has gained inspiration from his trips abroad – to places such as China, Japan and the Himalayas – and from the myths and legends of Cornwall.

How am I doing?

1 If a root ends in y, change the y to i and then add the suffix.
2 i before e except after c.
3 Possible answers include:
a **N**ever **E**at **C**hocolate **E**clairs **S**ince **S**ome **A**re **R**ather **Y**ucky / **O**ne **c**ollar and **t**wo **s**leeves.
b **B**abies **e**at **c**ustard **a**nd **u**ncles **s**uck **e**ggs.
4 **a** miniphoto / a small light **b** aerophobia / fear of air
c octology / study of the number 8 **d** autogram / a record of oneself
5 **a** fish **b** bat **c** hills **d** log
6 **a** snowed under **b** glistening jewel **c** monster
7 **a** true **b** false **c** false
8 **a** false **b** true
9 **a** ✓ **b** ✗
10 **a** ✗ **b** ✓
11 **a** The house was sold for double the amount that was paid for it.
b The project was completed two days before the deadline.
12 Before you start, ensure there is an adult with you. The aim is to find out if it takes twice as long to boil twice as much water.
1 First, pour enough water for 2 cups into a kettle.
2 Switch the kettle on and start the stopwatch.
3 As soon as the kettle boils, stop the watch and note the time.
4 Fill the kettle with enough water for 4 cups.
5 Switch the kettle on again and start the stopwatch.
6 Note down the time taken.
7 Compare with the result for 2 cups and draw your conclusion.

Contracting sentences

Grammar | Lesson 26

Some words in sentences are more important than others in conveying meaning:

- I __________ rock songs. Without a **verb**, a sentence does not make sense.
- __________ sing rock songs. Without a **pronoun**, a sentence sounds like an order!
- I sing rock __________. Without a **noun**, you do not have the full information.
- I was singing a __________ song. Removing **adjectives** or **adverbs** from sentences is less likely to alter the meaning of a sentence.

It is useful to remember the important parts of a sentence when shortening work.

1. Cross out all the non-essential words, without changing the basic meaning.

a Lots of sticky brown chocolate was smeared all over her chubby round cheeks.

b With long extended strides, the spotted cheetah raced after the small young zebra.

c The enormous black bear gently held the little tiny cub in its large padded paw.

2. Cross out words in this paragraph to keep the meaning while reducing its length. You should be able to reduce it to 23 words. *(4 marks)*

First and foremost it is always extremely important to shut and secure all wooden field gates. Never under any circumstances, pick, uproot or disturb any flowering plants or shrubs.

Any dogs that you have with you should be kept firmly on strong leads. Walk carefully and quietly to avoid undue disturbance to wildlife, birds and other animals.

3. Rewrite this paragraph in an even shorter form as very short notes. You don't need to use verbs when making notes. You can also abbreviate words. *(7 marks)*

Garbles are brown, hole-dwelling creatures whose main food is zat weed and bongo grass. They are nocturnal, only coming out after nightfall to visit the Darfar swamps where they swim and feed. The adult garble is two metres long, has ivory tusks and long ears. Baby garbles are born blind and only gain their sight after two weeks. The main enemy of the garble is the rocky eagle. It has a wing span of three metres, builds its nests in the Harfar mountains and has good night vision.

Garbles: brown, hole-dwelling. Food: ______________________________

____

0 — Tough — OK — Got it! — 14

Total /14

More practice? Go to www

Lesson 27 Grammar

Conditionals

Conditional sentences show **what could happen** (the result) if **a condition** or **event** happens first.

If it rains, we will stay in.

condition result

Conditional sentences include words and phrases such as:

if…then if…were would could provided that on condition that

1. Underline the conditional words or phrases in these sentences.

a If my skateboard is repaired in time then I can come too.

b Provided that James behaves himself he can play with my toys.

c We will go to the fair on condition that everyone stays together.

d They would buy a new house if they won the lottery.

e I would come with you if I could find my other shoe.

f Mum said we could go provided that we were home by eight o'clock.

2. Make full sentences using the conditional terms, conditions and results.

Conditional terms	Conditions	Results
If	this were a magic carpet	you could fall and break your leg
Provided that	you are not careful	I could fly away
If	I tidy my room	you can go to Terry's
Unless	you finish your homework	I cannot go to the cinema

a ______________________________

b ______________________________

c ______________________________

d ______________________________

0 Tough OK Got it! 10

Total

/10

More practice? Go to 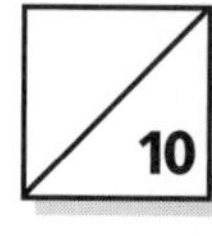

Apostrophes

Punctuation | Lesson 28

Apostrophes have two main uses.

They **replace missing letters** in **contractions**.

- I **had** = I'd.

They show **possession**.

- The bag belonging to the **girl**. — The girl**'s** bag.

The books belonging to the **children**. — The children**'s** books.

The bags belonging to the **girls**. — The girls**'** bags.

1. Rewrite these sentences using apostrophes where possible.

a It is no use, I cannot sleep. ______

b You should have said. I could have helped. ______

c They must not go, I have not said goodbye. ______

d "That is strange! Where is Tom?" ______

e Who has got a torch? It is dark in here! ______

2. Rewrite these phrases, using an apostrophe to show possession.

a The book belonging to Sophie. ______

b The tail belonging to the fox. ______

c The leg of the chair. ______

d The project belonging to Ranjit and Stuart. ______

3. Write in all the missing apostrophes in this passage. *(10 marks)*

We couldnt wait to get into Mums car. We left at 3 o clock and set off for Grandpas house. Dad agreed with Mums suggestion to drive through the villages, although we couldve taken the motorway. Wed have a more interesting journey that way. We passed Mr Jones sheep in the field. It was quite a long journey to Grandpas so I read some of my sisters book.

0 Tough OK Got it! 19

Total /19

More practice? Go to www

Lesson 29 Punctuation

Dialogue

Speech marks indicate **direct speech** in text. When a sentence of speech is **interrupted** by narrative, **commas** are used to show the interruption and the speech continues with a **small letter**. For example:

"If you want my opinion," said Julie, "**t**hat colour doesn't suit you at all!"

If a **new** sentence starts after the interruption, it begins with a capital letter.

"Where is Sanjay?" asked Keri. "**H**e was here a minute ago!"

1. Rewrite these sentences including the missing punctuation.

a Look the boy shouted Look up there

____

b Come here Tom demanded Dad and sort your room out

____

c Stop bellowed the policeman Stop at once

____

d Where on earth did I put my keys muttered Mum

____

2. Rewrite this passage correctly, adding in all the missing punctuation and capital letters. *(6 marks)*

mum called juhi yes replied mum whats the matter i cant find my school bag i have looked in my bedroom in your room and in rajs room but it doesnt seem to be here can you see it downstairs anywhere i havent noticed it down here said mum but ill have a look for you thanks mum youre the best shouted juhi

QUICK TIP!
Start a new line when a different character speaks.

____

____

____

____

0 Tough OK Got it! 10

Total /10

More practice? Go to www

Commas

Single commas are used to:

- separate items in a **list**. Apples, pears, bananas and grapes.
- separate **clauses** and **comments**. Although it was cold, he wore a T-shirt.
- **clarify** meaning in **ambiguous** phrases. Call me Sam. / Call me, Sam.

Pairs of commas are used to:

- **embed** a **subordinate clause** in a main clause.
  He said, although it wasn't true, that he'd flown to the Moon.
- separate **extra** (non-essential) **information** from the rest of a sentence.
  My Dad, who can do anything, told me that he could lift up an elephant.

1. Add the missing commas to these sentences.

a Mr Reeves handed out pens rulers individual whiteboards and cloths to the class.

b Despite the fact that she had a cold she was prepared to sing in the choir.

c Meanwhile back stage tension was mounting.

d Hans Christian Anderson the Danish writer is famous for his fairy tales.

e I wanted a bike a computer game some books and a pair of shoes for my birthday.

f William I known as William the Conqueror invaded England in 1066.

2. Put a comma in each of these sentences to remove the ambiguities.

a Outside the playground was empty.

b I want you to go with Mary Jamil.

c Michael and James the Peterson twins are rowing.

d For afternoon tea cakes and rolls were served.

3. Link each sentence to its implied meaning.

a My uncle Ted is a teacher.	Some animals are dangerous.
b My uncle, Ted, is a teacher.	Ted is one of my uncles.
c Animals which are dangerous are to be avoided.	All animals are dangerous.
d Animals, which are dangerous, are to be avoided.	My only uncle, Ted, is a teacher.

0 Tough OK Got it! 14

Total /14

More practice? Go to www

Lesson 31 Comprehension

Nonsense poetry

Nonsense poetry is poetry that is not serious. It tends to include:

- made up words
- a story that does not make proper sense
- a strong use of rhyme and alliteration.

The most famous writer of nonsense poetry is Edward Lear.

Read this poem by Edward Lear at least twice. Then answer the questions.

The Quangle Wangle's Hat

I

On the top of the Crumpetty Tree
The Quangle Wangle sat,
But his face you could not see,
On account of his Beaver Hat.
For his hat was a hundred and two feet wide,
With ribbons and bibbons on every side
And bells, and buttons, and loops, and lace,
So that nobody ever could see the face
Of the Quangle Wangle Quee.

II

The Quangle Wangle said
To himself on the Crumpetty Tree,—
'Jam; and jelly; and bread;
'Are the best food for me!
'But the longer I live on this Crumpetty Tree
'The plainer that ever it seems to me
'That very few people come this way
'And that life on the whole is far from gay!'
Said the Quangle Wangle Quee.

III

But there came to the Crumpetty Tree,
Mr. and Mrs. Canary;
And they said, — 'Did you ever see
'Any spot so charmingly airy?
'May we build a nest on your lovely Hat?
Mr. Quangle Wangle, grant us that!
'O please let us come and build a nest
'Of whatever material suits you best,
'Mr. Quangle Wangle Quee!'

IV

And besides, to the Crumpetty Tree
Came the Stork, the Duck, and the Owl;
The Snail, and the Bumble-Bee,
The Frog, and the Fimble Fowl;
(The Fimble Fowl, with a Corkscrew leg;)
And all of them said, — We humbly beg,
'We may build our homes on your lovely Hat,—
'Mr. Quangle Wangle, grant us that!
'Mr. Quangle Wangle Quee!'

V

And the Golden Grouse came there,
And the Pobble who has no toes,—
And the small Olympian bear,—
And the Dong with a luminous nose.
And the Blue Babboon, who played the flute,—
And the Orient Calf from the Land of Tute,—
And the Attery Squash, and the Bisky Bat,—
All came and built on the lovely Hat
Of the Quangle Wangle Quee.

VI

And the Quangle Wangle said
To himself on the Crumpetty Tree,—
'When all these creatures move
'What a wonderful noise there'll be!'
And at night by the light of the Mulberry moon
They danced to the flute of the Blue Babboon,
On the broad green leaves of the Crumpetty
Tree,
And all were as happy as happy could be,
With the Quangle Wangle Quee.

1. **Why was the Quangle Wangle Quee not happy?**

___

2. **What do we know about the hat?** *(3 marks)*

___

3. **Make a list of all the made-up animals in the poem.**

___

4. **What attracted the creatures to the tree?**

___

5. **Write down four pairs of words that alliterate in the poem.** *(4 marks)*

___

6. **Find an internal rhyme in the first verse of the poem.**

___

QUICK TIP!
Sometimes in poetry you get words that rhyme within a line: 'He had a fish on a dish'. These are called **internal rhymes**.

7. **Which of these phrases best describes the mood and rhythm of the poem? Circle one answer.**

sad and slow	exciting and rapid
happy and bouncy	frightening and heavy

8. **The poem has no real story yet it is enjoyable to read. Can you suggest why?**

___

___

0 Tough OK Got it! 13

Total /13

More practice? Go to www

Lesson 32 Comprehension

Balanced arguments

An argument is a **discussion** or **debate** in which people say what they think, either in **support** of or **against** a topic. Discussion texts aim to present a **balanced** view of all points surrounding a subject. An effective, balanced written argument might contain:

- a title in the form of a **question**
- **facts** or statistics and the **scope** of the argument in the introduction
- statements **for** and **against** the argument
- a **summary** at the end
- **debating terms** such as: some people believe… / it is undeniable that…
- use of **conditionals** where appropriate: would / could / should / might
- a logical structure, using **connectives**: furthermore / however / as a result.

Read this article, and then answer the questions.

Should children be made to wear school uniform?

Most pupils in the UK wear a school uniform. It is a tradition dating back to Tudor times. Some people believe that school uniform helps provide a positive way of reducing discipline problems and increasing school safety. Considerable debate has taken place over many years as to whether school uniform has now had its day.

Supporters of school uniform believe that normal clothes might be distracting to a pupil's studies and that the clothing could take attention away from the purpose of school. They state that pupils are more interested in clothing labels than work. On the other hand, many people would argue that pupils do not wear clothes in order to distract other pupils and would support this by asking if anyone has complained of being unable to do their work because someone's shirt was too bright.

While there are clearly many reasons why pupils might dislike school uniform, there are also many reasons why schools should have a school uniform. However, it is this writer's view that; it might now be time to provide uniforms that, while being hard-wearing and smart, do appeal more to those who have to wear them.

1. **What is the first fact introduced by the article?**

____

2. **Circle the connectives used in the article.** *(4 marks, ½ mark each)*

3. **Which debating terms are included in the article?** _______________

____

4. **Underline the conditional terms the author uses in the article.** *(4 marks)*

5. **What arguments are put forward supporting school uniform?** _______________

____

6. **What evidence is given to support this view?** _______________

____

7. **What arguments are put forward against wearing school uniform?** _______________

____

8. **What evidence is given to support this view?** _______________

____

9. **Does the writer include any personal opinions? Explain your answer.**

____

____

10. **Do you think this article presents a balanced argument? Why?**

____

____

0 Tough OK Got it! 16

Total /16

More practice? Go to www

How am I doing?

1. Rewrite these words correctly, putting in the missing unstressed letters.

a genrally ____________ **b** genrous ____________ **c** marrige ____________

d hankerchief ____________ **e** memrable ____________

2. Write two words that begin with each prefix.

a auto ____________ ____________

b tele ____________ ____________

c sub ____________ ____________

3. Complete each sentence with a word that begins with the prefix in brackets.

a I used a ________________ when I sang at the karaoke night. (micro)

b A message sent by telegraph is called a ________________. (tele)

c We sat in the front row of the ________________ and watched the show. (audi)

4. What do these Latin and Greek prefixes mean?

a circum ____________

b semi ____________

c micro ____________

5. Match the first part of these proverbs with the second part.

a A bad workman — is a penny gained.

b A fool and his money — less speed.

c A penny saved — always blames his tools.

d Everything must have — are soon parted.

e More haste — a beginning.

6. Change these sentences from active to passive.

a Mike broke the window. ________________________________

b They completed their maths homework. ________________________________

c Ranjna placed the crayons on the table. ________________________________

7. **Rewrite these phrases using imperatives.**

a Your dogs are not allowed in this hotel. ______________________________

b Parking is not permitted in this area. ______________________________

c Please do not do that. ______________________________

8. **Underline the subordinate clauses in these sentences.**

a "Before you sit down, can you pass me my cup of tea?"

b He went to the concert, even though he had a headache.

c While he was in Rome, he went to see an opera.

9. **Cross out all the non-essential words, without changing the basic meaning.**

a The cheerful, friendly waiter brought four bowls of delicious rosy red raspberries.

b The long-limbed giraffe stood next to his small, stumpy baby by the narrow stream.

c He put the heavy red book and bright blue folder on the large maple coffee table.

10. **Circle the conditional terms in these sentences.**

a If I won the competition, then I would organise a large party to celebrate.

b You could become unhealthy if you eat too much junk food.

c He could go home early provided that he finished his work first.

11. **Write in all the missing apostrophes in these sentences.**

a "Danny, isnt that your Dads new car? Or is it your Mums?"

b The book was Sallys but as she had read it she swapped it for Jess magazine.

c We cant go to the park as Rajs van wont start. Well have to stay in instead.

12. **Write all the missing punctuation into these sentences.**

a Lets go to the park Steve called over the fence to Roger Teds there already

b Gran, can we make some angel cakes asked Bella for Mums birthday

c Look at this mess bellowed Mr Jones Did you really need to do all this

Total

/40

More practice? Go to www

Lesson 33 Spelling

Spelling rules 1

The spelling of some root words **does not** change if a suffix is added:

wish **wish**ed

But the spelling of some other root words **does** have to be changed:

hop **hop**ped

There are **three** general rules for words whose spelling changes when a suffix is added.

1. What is the rule for words ending in e if the suffix begins with a vowel?

a ______________________________

ripe nice rude close white

Use the rule to add the suffix **er** to the words above.

b __________ **c** __________ **d** __________ **e** __________ **f** __________

2. What is the rule for words with a short vowel sound?

a ______________________________

plan let knit shop drum

Use the rule to add the suffix **ing** to the words above.

b __________ **c** __________ **d** __________ **e** __________ **f** __________

3. What is the rule for words ending in y?

a ______________________________

chilly tiny easy happy funny

Use the rule to add the suffix **est** to the words above.

b __________ **c** __________ **d** __________ **e** __________ **f** __________

4. Add the suffixes ful, less and fully to these words.

a care __________ __________ __________

b pity __________ __________ __________

c pain __________ __________ __________

0 Tough OK Got it! 21

Total

/21

More practice? Go to 

Spelling rules 2

Many singular nouns are made into plurals by just adding **s** or **es**:

book / books **brush / brushes**

But the spelling of some nouns must be **changed** before they are made plural:

story / stories

Many words have the common letter strings **ie** or **ei**. This rhyme explains which one to use:

Use i before e, except after c. When a or i is the sound, it's the other way round.

1. What is the rule for pluralising words ending in a consonant and y?

a ______________________________

berry family puppy sty party

Use the rule to pluralise the words above.

b __________ **c** __________ **d** __________ **e** __________ **f** __________

2. What is the rule for pluralising words ending in f or fe?

a ______________________________

knife loaf thief life shelf

Use the rule to pluralise the words above.

b __________ **c** __________ **d** __________ **e** __________ **f** __________

3. Use the i before e rule to check the spelling of these words. Tick the correct spellings and write the incorrect spellings correctly.

a mischeif __________ **b** deceive __________ **c** nieghbour __________

d freind __________ **e** hieght __________ **f** cieling __________

g kaliedoscope __________ **h** interview __________ **i** fierce __________

0 Tough OK Got it! 21

Total /21

More practice? Go to www

Lesson 35 Spelling

Mnemonics

A **mnemonic** (pronounced new-monic) is a verse or saying that helps you **remember** things.

Mnemonics can help with the spelling of tricky words by:

- spelling words in **full**: **C**an **a**n **u**gly **g**iraffe **h**ave **t**wins? (caught)
- emphasising **part** of a word: **Liam** became a Member of Par**liam**ent
- linking words that **share** common letter strings: The **medic** gave her the **medic**ine.

There are always different ways of remembering how to spell the same word:

necessary **N**ever **E**at **C**hocolate **E**clairs **S**ince **S**ome **A**re **R**ather **Y**ucky

One **c**ollar and **two s**leeves (one 'C', two 'S's).

1. Which words will these mnemonics help you to spell correctly?

a Blue elephants awaken under trees yawning. ________________

b Bears eat nearly every fish in trees. ________________

c Rhythm has your two hips moving. ________________

d Babies eat custard and uncles suck eggs. ________________

2. Complete the mnemonics using the words below.

separate busy psalm island

a An ____________ is land in water.

b The bus is ____________ .

c Peter said a long ____________ in church.

d There is a rat in ____________ .

3. Make up some of your own mnemonics for words you find difficult to spell.

a ____

b ____

c ____

d ____

0 Tough OK Got it! 12

Total

/12

More practice? Go to www

Inventing words

Spelling Lesson 36

New words are being invented all the time as we discover or invent new things.

A **microscope** was so named because it allows us to **look** (scope) at **very small** (micro) things.

If we know what a prefix or suffix means, we can use it to create words of our own.

1. **Write the meanings of these prefixes and suffixes.**

a phone ______ b ology ______ c graphy ______
d cede ______ e auto ______ f super ______
g bi ______ h phobia ______ i photo ______
j aero ______ k aqua ______ l gram ______

2. **Link these invented words with their meanings.**

a superphone	looks in two directions	b photology	to give way slightly
c autophobia	excessive sound	d microcede	the study of oneself
e biscope	writing about the air	f aquagram	the study of light
g aerography	a fear of one's self	h autology	a record of water

3. **Write the definitions of these words.**

a microperson = ______ b aquabiscuit = ______
c biface = ______ d octophone = ______
d autocleanse = ______ e triphobe = ______

4. **Invent new words using these prefixes and suffixes. Write their meanings.**

under post scape hood

a ______ means ______
b ______ means ______
c ______ means ______
d ______ means ______

0 Tough OK Got it! 30

Total /30

More practice? Go to www

Lesson 37 Spelling

Similes

Similes (pronounced sim-ill-lees) create a picture in the reader's mind by **comparing** one thing with another, usually to **exaggerate**:

The giant was **as big as a house**. The horse was **as white as snow**.

The avalanche rushed forward **like an express train**.

1. Complete the similies using these words.

weather mule arrow ABC drowned rat

a Gavin could be as stubborn as a ________________ when it suited him.

b The flight of the ball was as swift as an ________________ .

c Stuart came in from the rain looking like a ________________ .

d Lorna was as uncertain as the ________________ about the idea.

e Once he had read the instructions it was as simple as ________________ .

2. Underline the similes in this piece of writing.

We were packed as quick as a flash and as happy as larks to be leaving this place. The luggage was stacked like building blocks in the foyer. We were as brown as berries from the Sun but were as pleased as punch to be moving on.

3. Complete the similes using different words from the usual ones given in brackets.

a as quiet as ____________ (a mouse)

b as tough as ____________ (nails)

c as bright as ____________ (a button)

d as strong as ____________ (an ox)

e run like ____________ (the wind)

f as thick as ____________ (thieves)

4. Use your own endings to complete these similes.

a It was as cheap as ____________ .

b The plant was as dead as ____________ .

c It was as smooth as ____________ .

d His brain was as sharp as ____________ .

e Her feet were as warm as ____________ .

f He was as sly as ____________ .

0 Tough OK Got it! 18

Total /18

More practice? Go to www

Metaphors

A **metaphor** describes something as if it is something else, suggesting **similarities** but not comparing things in the way that similes do. Metaphors help to create a vivid picture for the reader and make narrative and poetry much more interesting:

His daughter was the **apple** of his eye.

1. Underline the metaphors in these sentences.

a "Your bedroom is a tip!" shouted Mum.

b Her eyes were pools of chocolate.

c "Sorry I'm late, the traffic was murder!"

d He had a heart of stone.

e The garden is a small wilderness.

2. Complete each metaphor with the appropriate word or phrase below.

red-handed green carpet thorny little monkey ball of flames

a The grass was a ____________________.

b He was caught ____________________.

c Soon after the fire started the house was a ____________________.

d Her son was a ____________________ on Saturday!

e It was a ____________________ question.

3. Think of your own metaphors to complete these sentences.

a The snow is ____

b Grandpa said that life is a ____

c The Sun is ____

d Love is ____

0 Tough OK Got it! 14

Total /14

More practice? Go to www

Lesson 39 Grammar

Narrative texts

The voice describing the events in a text is called the **narrator**. We read from the narrator's viewpoint; how he or she sees it.
When the narrator is part of the story, it is written in the **first person**.
When the narrator is not part of the story, it is written in the **third person**.

1. Decide whether these statements about narrative texts are true or false.

a Narrative texts are always written in the present tense. ______

b A piece of descriptive writing always starts a narrative text. ______

c A narrative text usually has a beginning, middle and end. ______

d The author of a narrative text is always the narrator of the story. ______

e Narrative texts have no more than two characters. ______

f Openings of narrative texts can be a few lines or two or three paragraphs. ______

2. Rewrite this narrative extract in the third person (from the point of view of someone watching what was happening). *(7 marks)*

I was swimming when suddenly Jason bombed me. He had leapt off the side, tucked up his knees, wrapped his arms round them and landed in the pool with an almighty splash – right on top of me. It forced me under the water. I was coughing and choking. "Somebody help me!"

Somebody did. Hands reached out, pulled me to the surface and helped me out of the pool – Jason's.

"I'm sorry Trudy. I didn't see you there. I was just larking about."

"Well, next time, look first. You could have hurt me, I could have drowned," I shouted, half in anger, half in fright.

Trudy was swimming ______

______

______

______

______

______

0 Tough OK Got it! 13

Total /13

More practice? Go to www

Instructional texts 1

Instructions and directions are best written in a clear, compact style. They should use just enough words to keep them clear and understandable, while providing all the essential information.

1. Circle the features that are most useful in an instructional text.

numbered points chapters diagrams conclusion step-by-step details

2. Decide whether these statements about instructional texts are true or false.

a Instructional texts should be written in clear, precise language. ____________

b Any adverbs in instructional texts should be chosen for their vividness, not clarity. ____________

c Instructional texts are often written in the first person singular. ____________

d Instructional texts usually start by stating the aim of the instructions. ____________

e Information in instructional texts is often organised using bullet points. ____________

f Numbered lists are never used in instructional texts. ____________

g A fictional story is an example of an instructional text. ____________

3. Read these instructions for finding synonyms in a book in the library then rewrite them more clearly and concisely, removing any unnecessary information. Think carefully about the way in which instructions are usually presented. *(8 marks)*

Go to the library upstairs. You'll like it up there because there are so many books! The section for dictionaries is at the far end on your left. On the second shelf you will find a SAWF (a synonym, antonym and word finder) – it seems a very strange name for a book. Look up the word you need. Make a note of suitable synonyms. Then look up some of the synonyms for those words too because they might be more suitable.

____

____

____

____

0 Tough OK Got it! 16

Total /16

More practice? Go to www

Lesson 41 Grammar

Persuasive texts

Persuasive writing is written with the aim of changing other people's views – not always a very easy task!

Effective persuasive writing is often a combination of appeals to our **emotions** (feelings and reactions) and our **head** (logic and argument).

1. Circle the features you would expect to find in a persuasive text.

opinion   powerful adjectives   chapters   powerful verbs   table of contents

2. Decide whether these statements about persuasive texts are true or false.

a Persuasive texts offer objective points of view. ____________

b Persuasive texts often include phrases of exaggeration. ____________

c The key issue of a persuasive text is usually detailed in the opening phrases. ____________

d Rhetorical questions are not used in persuasive writing. ____________

e Persuasive texts only present facts about an issue or topic. ____________

f Persuasive texts often disguise opinion as fact. ____________

g Persuasive texts aim to provoke an emotional response from the reader. ____________

h Persuasive texts often repeat key facts and arguments. ____________

i Persuasive texts always present a complete and fully supported argument. ____________

3. Tick these sentences if you think they come from persuasive texts.

a In Cambridge there are 42 zebra crossings to make the city safer for pedestrians. ____

b Washo washing powder works on your clothes like a white whirlpool. Why use anything else? ____

c Surveys show that nearly all pet owners who really care for their dogs choose Fido. ____

d An RSPCA report stated that 80 per cent of dog owners feed their pets canned dog food. ____

e The National Democrats – the only party that really supports hard-up pensioners. ____

0 Tough   OK   Got it! 15

Total /15

More practice? Go to www

Impersonal writing

Impersonal texts
- offer **facts** rather than personal opinions
- are often written in the **passive** voice
- contain **imperative verbs**
- do not use personal pronouns such as I or you.

'I think you turn left at the post office' is a **personal** statement.
'Turn left at the post office' is an **impersonal** statement.
Explanatory texts and non-chronological reports are examples of texts that use impersonal writing.

1. Put a tick next to the sentences that have come from impersonal texts.

a The car was driven down the road at great speed. ________

b I believe the train has arrived already. ________

c You will agree with me when you have read the rest of this article. ________

d Tennis was introduced to England during the 14th century. ________

e Bengal tigers have been living in India for many years. ________

2. Rewrite this passage as a piece of impersonal text. *(5 marks)*

I filled the kettle with water and switched it on. I cut the jelly into cubes and placed them in a measuring jug. I allowed the kettle to almost boil and then poured water onto the jelly cubes until it reached 500 ml. I stirred it until the jelly had dissolved. I then left it until I could comfortably touch the jug. I poured the jelly into a dish and left it in a cool place until it was cold then I put it in the fridge until it was set.

Fill the kettle with water ____

____

____

____

____

____

0 Tough OK Got it! 10

Total /10

More practice? Go to www

Lesson 43 Grammar

Paragraphs

Paragraphs are a form of punctuation. They show how sentences are grouped together. A new paragraph is marked by a new line that starts about a finger's width in from the edge.

Paragraphs are used to mark:
- the opening of the writing
- a new thought, aspect or idea in the writing
- dialogue spoken by a new speaker.

1. Read the beginning of this old Chinese tale, then explain why a new paragraph was started in each section.

a One day a tiger came upon a fox. The fox looked most appetising so the tiger prepared to leap on the fox and devour him.

b "Take care, my friend," warned the fox, "you don't understand. I have been appointed King of the Beasts. If you touch a hair on my head you will be punished."

c The tiger roared with laughter. "You? The King of the Beasts Ha Ha!" The tiger…

a ______________________________

b ______________________________

c ______________________________

2. Read this part of a story then rewrite it, setting it out in paragraphs. *(4 marks)*

Jenny slumped down in her seat. Why did boys always have the luck? Why couldn't girls have some too? Her mind was running round in circles. "Go on then, Jenny love." Her father's voice broke into her thoughts. "What is it?" "It's the girls' turn now. You do want a ride on that elephant, don't you?"

____

____

____

____

____

0 Tough OK Got it! 7

Total /7

More practice? Go to www

Formal letters

Formal letters are written for many reasons, for example: to **request** more information, to **complain** or to **explain** something. Despite their different purposes, all these letters have **similar layouts** and **features**.

1. Circle the appropriate ways to begin formal letters.

a Dear Sir, **b** hiya Gramps **c** Dear Amy White, **d** Hello Sam **e** Dear Mr Cox,

What do the ones you've circled have in common?

____

2. Circle the appropriate ways to end formal letters.

a Yours faithfully, **b** TTFN **c** cheers **d** Respectfully yours, **e** Yours sincerely,

What do the ones you've circled have in common?

____

3. Are these statements about formal letters true or false?

a The sender's address is always written in the top left-hand corner. __________

b The recipient's name and address are written on the right-hand side. __________

c The addresses do not need any forms of punctuation. __________

d The content of a formal letter should be written in one long paragraph. __________

e The content should be written in a logical order and should follow the standard rules for punctuating sentences. __________

f Paragraph indents are never used in formal letters. __________

4. You are working on a project. Write a formal letter to the French Tourist Board asking for information on Paris: how to get there, accommodation, transport, what to see, where to eat. Remember to introduce yourself, explain why you are writing and use correct punctuation.

Use a separate sheet of paper.

0 Tough OK Got it! 17

Total /17

More practice? Go to www

Lesson 45 Punctuation

Playscripts

A playscript is made up of the characters' lines and the moves they have to make on the stage.

To write a playscript:

- the setting must be carefully described
- use a colon after a person's name and punctuate what they say
- start a new line when another actor speaks
- put the stage direction for the moves of the characters in brackets
- write words as they should be spoken – 'I don't know' or 'dunno'.

Read the beginning of a scene from this playscript.

(Simon and Dave, two ten-year-old boys are in bed. Simon hears something and reaches across to wake up his brother.)

Simon: Dave, Wake up! (He shakes him again.) Wake up!
Dave: Wha' suh matter? (Dave struggles to sit up.)
Simon: Ssh! Listen! (They both appear to be listening) Did you hear that?

1. Describe the setting in detail – what the stage looks like and what is on the stage.

The scene is ______________________________

____

____

2. Write what happens next in this scene. Put the stage directions in brackets.

Dave: ______________________________

____

____

____

____

____

____

0 Tough	OK	Got it! 2

Total /2

More practice? Go to www

Instructional texts 2

Punctuation | Lesson 46

Imagine it is your birthday and you are having a party. Decide the details of where and when it will be celebrated. Make sure that you punctuate your invitation, the directions and your thank you letter correctly.

1. Write down the following information:

What date is your party? ______________________________

Where is it to be held? ______________________________

What time should your guests arrive? _______ What time should they be collected? _______

Do they need to bring anything? ______________________________

What should they wear? ______________________________

2. Write an invitation to your birthday, include all the above information.

____

____

____

____

3. Write directions for getting from school to where the party is being held.

____

____

____

____

4. Write a short 'thank you' letter to one of your friends who came to your party.

____

____

____

____

0 Tough OK Got it! 4

Total

/4

More practice? Go to www

Lesson 47 Comprehension

Comparing poems

There are many varieties of poems, for example: **narrative poems**, **shape poems**, **haiku**, **sonnets** and **limericks**. Each of these types of poem has different features and layouts, but they often cover similar themes. It is often interesting to compare poems by:

type of poem **subject** **strengths** and **weaknesses** **mood appeal** to the reader

Read the two poems below and then answer the questions.

A

Sea Fever

I must go down to the seas again, to the lonely sea and the sky,
And all I ask is a tall ship and a star to steer her by,
And the wheel's kick and the wind's song and the white sail's shaking,
And a grey mist on the sea's face and a grey dawn breaking.

I must go down to the seas again, for the call of the running tide
Is a wild call and a clear call that may not be denied;
And all I ask is a windy day with the white clouds flying,
And the flung spray and the blown spume, and the sea-gulls crying.

I must go down to the seas again, to the vagrant gypsy life,
To the gull's way and the whale's way, where the wind's like a whetted knife;
And all I ask is a merry yarn from a laughing fellow-rover,
And quiet sleep and a sweet dream when the long trick's over.

John Masefield

B

Disevolving

As a child it was fun
To spring from the towels, aiming straight at the sea,
And have it wrestle with me,
My quick stride quenched to slow-motion,
Until – at waist high –
I could make better going
By lifting up horizontal
And flapping my limbs
Fish-wise.

Joseph Johnson

1. **What is the difference between the rhymes in the two poems?**

____

2. **What is the central theme (subject) of both of these poems?**

____

3. **Decide which of the poems each of these statements refers to. Say whether each statement is a strength or a weakness.**

   a The poem has a strong, clear rhythm in each verse. ___ strength / weakness

   b When read aloud, it isn't clear that it has been written as a poem. ___ strength / weakness

   c An effective description of what it is like to be in the water. ____ strength / weakness

   d It contains old English terms which can be difficult to understand. ____ strength / weakness

4. **What mood or emotions do you feel each poem creates in the reader?** *(2 marks)*

   Poem A ____

   ____

   Poem B ____

   ____

5. **What do you think will appeal to the reader about each poem?** *(2 marks)*

   Poem A ____

   ____

   Poem B ____

   ____

6. **Which poem appeals to you most? Explain your answer.**

____

____

____

0 Tough OK Got it! 11

Total /11

More practice? Go to www

Lesson 48 Comprehension

Skimming and scanning

To swiftly determine what a text is about, it is useful to **skim read** the content. Skimming provides you with an **overview** and a general sense of the **main ideas** in a text. Reading elements such as a **title**, **headings**, **introduction** and **conclusion**, will quickly show if a text is relevant and should be read more closely.

To quickly find a specific piece of information, it is useful to **scan** the content. Scanning allows you to focus closely on the **key details** that are important to you.

You do not read every word or sentence with these techniques. You may find it useful to **underline** key terms or phrases as you skim or scan a text.

Skim read the title and headings of this passage and then answer questions 1 to 3.

Michael Foreman

He wrote and published his first book while he was still at art school. Now, Michael Foreman is one of the world's leading illustrators.

Background

Michael was born in Pakefield, Suffolk in 1938. As he grew up in wartime Britain, he read magazines, delivered newspapers and dreamed of being a footballer. At the age of 15, he went to art school and from there his natural talent was nurtured.

Career

Over his career, he has worked on magazines, book jackets and TV commercials and he has even designed Christmas stamps! However, Michael is best known for his illustrations – he has created illustrations for over 100 books for authors such as Roald Dahl and has also written and illustrated 30 of his own stories. His talent has been frequently recognised with prizes such as the Kate Greenaway Award.

Inspirational sources

Throughout his career, Michael has travelled widely to places such as China, Japan and the Himalayas and it is from these experiences that he has gained much of his inspiration for the settings and illustrations in his work. He also takes much of his inspiration from the myths and legends of Cornwall – where he and his family have a second home – and enjoys spending much of his time by the sea. His love of the ocean is clearly shown in the range of blues used in his artwork.

1. **What is the topic of this text?** ______

2. **From a quick skim, does the text give you the following information?**

   a Who his best friend was at school? ______

   b The grades he got at school? ______

   c What types of jobs he has had? ______

3. **Which section is likely to hold the most interesting information?**

______

Now scan the extract briefly, underline any key points and answer these questions.

4. **What is Michael Foreman's job?** ______

5. **When and where was he born?** ______

6. **What else has he designed apart from book jackets and magazines?**

______

7. **How many books has he illustrated for other authors?** ______

8. **How many books has Michael written?** ______

9. **How has his talent been rewarded?** ______

10. **Where does Michael get his inspiration from?**

______

______

______

0 Tough	OK	Got it! 12

Total

/12

More practice? Go to www

How am I doing?

1. **Which rule was applied to these words before the suffixes were added?**

   funniest cheeriest friendliest prettiest cheekiest

   ____

2. **Which rule do these words follow?**

   chief receive sieve grief deceit

   ____

3. **Write a mnemonic you know or make one up to help you remember these spellings.**

   a necessary ______________________________

   b because ______________________________

4. **Link these invented words with their definitions.**

a miniphoto	fear of the air
b aerophobia	a record of oneself
c octology	study of the number 8
d autogram	a small light

5. **Complete these similes using one of the nouns below.**

   bat log fish hills

   a Ravi swam like a ________.

   b Without his glasses, he was as blind as a ________.

   c That joke was as old as the ________.

   d Dad slept like a ________.

6. **Complete each metaphor with the appropriate word or phrase below.**

   snowed under monster glistening jewel

   a Sally was ____________ with work.

   b The Moon is a ____________.

   c Their boss is a ____________!

7. **Are these statements about narrative texts true or false?**

a Every narrative text has a narrator. ____________

b A piece of narrative text always starts with a section of dialogue. ____________

c Narrative texts are separated into scenes. ____________

8. **Are these statements about instructional texts true or false?**

a The purpose of an instructional text is to recount an event. ____________

b Instructional texts are written in the second person. ____________

9. **Tick the sentence which has been taken from a persuasive text.**

a 42 species of wildflower, three rare species of moth and eight different fungi live on Chartheath Common – it's a great place to get close to nature. ____________

b 42 species of wildflower, three rare species of moth and eight different fungi live on the Chartheath Common. ____________

10. **Tick the impersonal sentence.**

a She placed the saucer above the flame and saw the chemical reaction happen. ____________

b Press the red button on the remote control and hold for ten seconds. ____________

11. **Rewrite these sentences in the passive voice.**

a I sold the house for double the amount I paid for it.

____

b We completed the project two days before the deadline.

____

12. **Rewrite these instructions clearly, using appropriate punctuation.**

before you start ensure there is an adult with you the aim is to find out if it takes twice as long to boil twice as much water first pour enough water for 2 cups into a kettle switch the kettle on and start the stopwatch as soon as the kettle boils stop the watch and note the time fill the kettle with enough water for 4 cups switch the kettle on again and start the stopwatch note down the time taken compare with the result for 2 cups and draw your conclusion

____

____

____

Total

/ 27

More practice? Go to www